"Over the past twenty years, I have exposed, in two-week study tours, several hundred persons from different economic and religious backgrounds to the reality of poverty in the Caribbean and Central America. The traumatic impact of that experience radically altered the values of many of them. Such short immersion, however, can be no more than a start, as Bill and Patty Coleman demonstrate by their poignant account of two years' immersion in the lives and living conditions of Mexican slum dwellers.

"*Whispers of Revelation* is a beautiful story, full of enrichments and illuminations; perhaps the most important of these, for the authors and for the reader, is that the poorer people are, they harder they must work and the less they achieve. The miracle is that they continue to hope."

Gary MacEoin

"It has been 30 years since I first set foot in Latin America. I was anxious to see how the Colemans, *gringos* like me following a similar path, might react. I smiled, I wept, I laughed, I grew nostalgic as I read of 'Patty' and 'Memo' embarking on this cross-cultural journey.

"Read on if you'd like to experience the love, the laughter, the sorrow, and the pain: the life of the poor in Latin America. The questions the Colemans ask are difficult ones. The answers are, too. Read on to come to love the Latins—and the Colemans as well.

"They trace with a sure hand the story of their journey into the world of the poor in Mexico. With open hears and minds, they come to understand the Mexicans and to love them in the process. Love and understanding are contagious....So is joy."

Dan Jensen, M.M.
Veteran missioner in Latin America

"*Whispers of Revelation* is the spiritual adventure of two remarkable Americans, Patty and Bill Coleman, who set out to find the spirit of the poor in Cuernavaca, Mexico.

"Yesterday I returned from Cuernavaca. I saw the Colemans in action. We visited the poor ghetto areas so graphically described in the book—La Nopalera and Primera de Mayo—and witnessed the loving and spiritual relationship between the Mexican poor and the Colemans. The book, in part, is the culmination of an effort by four Vermonters—Bill and Patty, Jane Newton, and myself—who founded Vamos Vermont Associates to supply materials to help Mexicans help themselves with money raised in the U.S. Bill and Patty are our representatives in Mexico.

"*Whispers of Revelation* is a unique story of devotion to the Mexican poor, a story of Bill and Patty's search for the spirit of the poor. I believe they have embraced it."

Isaac Patch
President of Vamos

"What makes this book so valuable is the way in which the Colemans share the excitement of their journey with us. Their searching, their stumbling, and their learning are guided by a sense of thirst in their lives. They are led to an encounter with the poor and believing people of Mexico, which becomes an encounter with the God of the poor. Meeting these people in these pages, we are drawn into an encounter ourselves, which can help us to see our own lives, faith, and connectedness in a new light."

The Benedictine Monks of Weston Priory
Weston, Vermont

"The Coleman's odyssey to own the spirit of the poor is an invitation to all to look at their lives, reflect on them, and then act to bring about justice for all. Their simple but profound story disturbs the complacency and regularity of lives that seem to be going nowhere. Their challenge to work at bringing about God's kingdom pleads for a response."

Loretta Girzaitis
Co-author of *Still on the Cross*

DISCOVERING
THE SPIRIT OF THE POOR

Whispers of Revelation

BILL AND PATTY COLEMAN

TWENTY-THIRD PUBLICATIONS
Mystic, Connecticut 06355

Twenty-Third Publications
185 Willow Street
P.O. Box 180
Mystic, CT 06355
(203) 536-2611
800-321-0411

ISBN 0-89622-505-4
Library of Congress Catalog Card No 91-67644

Art credit Cover and title page: The Blaze (1933) by Maximo Pacheco,
Night Workers' Center, Atzcapotzalco, Mexico

Preface

Recently we moved from the United States to Cuernavaca, Mexico, in search of an elusive goal, a new understanding of God, which we hoped we would find among the Third World poor. This book is the story of our adventure: the people who taught us truths we would not have otherwise learned; the events that excited and sometimes terrified us, the ideas that came slowly to birth along the way.

These two years have been the most intense of our lives. We trust that we have done them justice in these pages and that they will awaken in you something of the excitement of discovery that has created in us new minds and new hearts.

Mexico is an oppressed country. A brave and outspoken Mexican bishop has called its government the most repressive in all of Latin America, and Amnesty International has documented its human rights abuses. The poor know all this; they often touch their right eye with an extended forefinger and say, *El gobierno es muy listo* (The government is always alert). For their safety, we have changed the names of many of the people we met and omit here the names of others we wish to thank. God knows their names and how grateful we are.

Among those we can name and wish to thank are the Guadalupan Missionaries of Christ the King who first introduced us to the Mexican poor eight years ago and who guided and encouraged us in our journey. The poor people of La Nopalera and Primero de

Mayo were our teachers and we will always be in their debt. Many others in Cuernavaca welcomed us, shared their knowledge, and helped us along the way.

Special thanks to our daughter Angel, who works as a Maryknoll lay missioner in Brazil, for helping us universalize our ideas and question our insights. Thanks, too, to the rest of our family for their unquestioning encouragement and support, especially Bill's eighty-four-year-old mother, Ethel, who journeyed to Cuernavaca and hugged and kissed our poor friends in La Nopalera.

Thanks to the monks of Weston Priory and our many friends in Weston, Vermont, who have helped in many remarkable ways and have themselves become involved in the lives of our poor friends.

Finally, we must express profound gratitude to Robert S. Gillcash, M.D., of Franklin, Connecticut, whose wisdom and healing touch helped Patty regain her health so she could make the journey here.

Come with us now as we set out for a land you may never have seen, and savor with us the richness of the poor.

Dedication

For the poor of La Nopalera and Primero de Mayo,
our teachers and our friends.

Contents

Whispers of Revelation

*"Happy are those who have
the spirit of the poor...."*

- BIENAVENTURADOS
  LOS QUE TIENEN ESPIRITU DE POBRE
  PORQUE DE ELLOS ES EL REINO DE LOS CIELOS

- BIENAVENTURADOS LOS MANSOS
  PORQUE ELLOS HEREDARAN LA TIERRA

- BIENAVENTURADOS LOS QUE LLORAN
  PORQUE ELLOS SERAN CONSOLADOS

- BIENAVENTURADOS LOS QUE TIENEN HAMBRE
  Y SED DE JUSTICIA
  PORQUE ELLOS SERAN SACIADOS

- BIENAVENTURADOS LOS MISERICORDIOSOS
  PORQUE ELLOS ALCANZARAN MISERICORDIA

- BIENAVENTURADOS LOS LIMPIOS DE CORAZON
  PORQUE ELLOS VERAN A DIOS

- BIENAVENTURADOS LOS QUE HACEN LA PAZ
  PORQUE ELLOS SERAN LLAMADOS:
  "HIJOS DE DIOS"

- BIENAVENTURADOS
  LOS PERSEGUIDOS POR ATENERSE A LO QUE ES JUSTO
  PORQUE DE ELLOS ES EL REINO DE LOS CIELOS

Wall plaque in Cuernavaca cathedral

Introduction

This is the story of an adventure, the kind that was once celebrated in ancient tales like *The Holy Grail, The Golden Fleece,* or even *The Odyssey.* It is the reality Jesus hinted at when he told the parable about "The Pearl of Great Price."

Our story is a classic one, a search against great odds for a treasure: a revelation strong enough to change our lives and to open new insights in the minds and hearts of those who hear it. This may sound romantic, but there are two problems to bring to your attention. The first is that we, the searchers, look more like Ma and Pa Kettle than Charlton Heston. The second is that the forces of evil that tried to hide the revelation from us, far from being demon dragons, are those perfectly reasonable North American assumptions we are all quite sure are correct.

Ours is an unlikely story but one worth telling because there are more Kettles than Hestons in the world and revelations can come to people of any age, your age or ours. Since you will be sharing our adventure, let us tell you a little about ourselves, and then say a word about revelation—for it was a revelation we were seeking—and about poverty.

A Word About Us
How do you decide to set off on an adventure when there is more of your life setting behind you than racing out in front? For us, this quest was an idea that had simmered in our hearts for years.

We had met and married while struggling for the rights of black people in the Civil Rights Movement in the southern United States. We had worked in soup kitchens, in the peace movement, and in solidarity with Central Americans. Yet, these experiences had only whetted our appetite for something more. Now that our children were adults with lives of their own, we had the freedom to set off on the adventure that had lingered in our hearts for over twenty years.

We were not completely unprepared for this adventure, since we had long been religious writers who knew the basic ins and outs of traditional and contemporary theology. We had written religion texts for teenagers, books and newsletters for those in pastoral ministry, and had lectured in different parts of the world on topics such as prayer, catechetics, and family.

We are in our fifties and there is no decade in one's life that lacks glamor any more than this one. The fifties may be a time when many people achieve power and "success," but they are hardly a time of excitement and promise. These are the years that convince the most stubborn of us that our youth has ended and that our bodies are not immortal as we had once imagined they are. These are the years, too, when bifocals replace our reading glasses, when our trips to the dentist become more involved and always more expensive, when our life insurance rates soar and many of our contemporaries give up the battle and die without consulting us at all. Some say that this is the age when we reach the zenith of our accomplishments, but those of us who have achieved anything worthwhile know that the end of it all is finally beginning. No, there is not much glamor left.

Yet, there was a ray of hope for us in the writing of Robert Bly, the author of *Iron John,* a study of the ancient fairy tales and their importance in understanding human growth. Bly, at least, had something good to say about being fifty:

> Time moves more swiftly in a fairy tale than with us, and
> the man in earth time would be about fifty years old now, or

older. Some flower has finally unfolded and blossomed....Fairy tales say that we each bring with us at birth
certain golden rings or spindles or memories of glory that
assure us we have a transcendent or grand side. But life in a
family takes that out of one fast and each of us goes through
a shaming time or deprivation time....

But all during that time, if we are lucky, the bridge is being rebuilt. Who has the design, who the architect is, who
makes the bricks or the steel beams, no one knows for sure,
and it is different for each person anyway. But, eventually, at
fifty or fifty-five, we feel a golden ring on the finger again.[1]

Notwithstanding the wisdom of the old tales, we were told repeatedly that being in our fifties was the wrong time to set off on
a great adventure. This decade is supposed to be a time for con-
solidating power, preparing for retirement, and enjoying our
grandchildren, not for starting life all over again. This advice
sounded good but we did not listen. Instead, we sold our business
and started off in quest of that elusive revelation we knew was
somewhere in our future.

A Word About Revelation
Revelation is one of those "churchy" words from which all the excitement has been carefully drained. It was not always this way.
The word was born in the Middle East and was a part, an exciting
part, of the marriage process. In past ages and in some places
even today, women live behind veils. No man was allowed to see
their faces, let alone their naked bodies. To lounge in a bikini on a
beach was unthinkable.

Courtship then as now began with some mutual interest which
was then formalized by negotiations between the families of the
man and woman who wanted to marry. Once the negotiations
were complete, the marriage was formalized before the community. Yet, the man still had not seen the woman's face. That came on
the first night they spent together. She removed her veils and her

other clothing and they stood naked together. This was the moment ancients called the "revelation," an exciting idea, certainly!

When people first told stories about Moses and the burning bush or the consuming furnace Abraham saw, they were hinting at the familiar idea of revelation that every married couple remembered so vividly. God was stripping the veils from self and standing naked and vulnerable to human gaze. It was a breathtaking event.

Much, much later when the scribes got hold of these stories they drained them of their energy and insisted that saying the proper words and participating in the right liturgies was the same thing as seeing God face to face. Thus, institutional religion was born.

We knew the words and had for years participated in the liturgies. Now it was time to see God face to face, so to speak, to experience a true revelation. This was why we had come to Mexico, the goal of the final years of our lives. We were ready for the adventure to begin.

A Word About Poverty

Many of our North American friends, especially those who had read widely and considered themselves social critics, warned us not to idealize poverty. We took this suggestion seriously, for there is nothing romantic about people living in poverty. When you have seen a mother weeping over her dead child who, with even elementary medical care, could have lived, you know that the life of the poor is anything but romantic.

There was, however, another warning implied in the first: "Be careful you do not idealize the poor." This was a problem that haunted us as we came to share more and more of our lives with them. We felt drawn into their mysterious way of coping with life's outrages and detected in them a nobility of character that was missing from our lives and those of our well-educated, affluent North American friends. For us there was an irresistible goodness in the poor and we were not sure what to make of it.

The possibility of idealizing the poor remained a problem until we discussed it with Bill's brother, a lifelong activist in the cause of the poor. He smiled at our confusion. "It seems to me that Jesus idealized the poor. He even said that we would be happy only if we became like them. What was good enough for him ought to be right for us."

So if you think we have idealized the poor in these pages, know that we are aware of it and are happy we did.

—Chapter One—

Rediscovering an Ancient Truth

*Saddled with all the limitations of middle age, we set
out on our adventure and find an exciting new truth, a
revelation with the power to change our lives.*

In October 1989, we prepared to cut our ties and set out on our
adventure, our own search for the Holy Grail. The story of our adventure was going to be a story different from the old myths or
from the stories of Abraham or Moses. We understood that.

Yet, we were more excited than even we would have thought
possible. We felt that mysterious fluid coursing through our bodies as we walked hand in hand through an unfamiliar Mexican
city. We had cut our ties with the past and here we were, unsure
of where we were going or what we were about to do. We knew
only that we had come to Mexico searching for some new vision
of God, a vision we were convinced we would find here. Precisely
how or where, we had no idea, but we were sure the search
would change our lives. As it turned out, it did.

Our First Discovery

An American Airlines jet deposited us in Mexico City, where we hurried through customs and met a friend who whisked us from Mexico City fifty miles south to Cuernavaca, a mountain city of about a million people. The five bags we carried were important—they contained our worldly possessions, at least all those on this side of the Rio Grande.

On this first full day of our adventure we set out to discover something about our new home. Cuernavaca, people said, had been a quiet little resort town even twenty years ago when hundreds of thousands of poor peasants began leaving their failed farms and migrating to the cities in search of work. Like all Latin American cities, Cuernavaca is a study in contrasts. It boasts over a thousand swimming pools, hundreds of thousands of weekend tourists from Mexico City, impressive formal gardens, enchanting restaurants, and more than thirty Spanish language schools for wealthy North Americans. But there is more to Cuernavaca than meets the tourist's eye, for most of the people live in unbelievable squalor hidden in the ravines, the railroad yards, and the "ring of death," the desperately poor neighborhoods that surround the city.

The city has a fascinating past—pre-Columbian ruins, Spanish fortresses, ancient sugar cane haciendas, old monasteries, and tales of the famous "India Bonita," the lover of the Emperor Maximilian. Early in this century, it was the center of Emiliano Zapata's revolutionary forces; older people still remember the heroics of Zapata's rag-tag army.

The tour guides insisted that we see the cathedral, one of Cuernavaca's impressive ties to its colonial past. We were not at all sure we wanted to see any more cathedrals, since we had spent our adult lives around churches, and one church, we had learned, was pretty much the same as another. Most of them were, we had often said, more a monument to someone's determination and pride than to a deep faith in God. Cathedrals, like the old forts, were more a symbol of control and power than of love and faith.

What changed our minds was the presence of a wonderful pizza parlor across the street from the cathedral compound. Bill loved pizza, and visiting the cathedral on the way to the pizza parlor made more sense than a visit to the cathedral alone.

As we approached the complex of churches, we were convinced that a visit would only confirm our skepticism about these ancient structures. A high wall with pointed battlements set five feet apart gave the impression of an ancient fortress where God protected self and Spanish friends against the onslaughts of the "savage" Indians. Some of the descendants of these Indians were gathered at the fortress door, not to engage in revolutionary slaughter, but to try to sell everything from miniature violins to garish copies of the miraculous image of Our Lady of Guadalupe. We clutched our traveler's checks in our pockets and rushed past.

Inside the walls there were, to our chagrin, more Indians, more items for sale, and three churches beckoning us to enter. We knew from our travels to other parts of the world that the Spanish loved churches; they seemed to believe that God needed as many homes as possible. Although there must have been homelessness in Cuernavaca, it did not appear that God had that problem.

It seemed perfectly reasonable to join a group of tourists who were "doing" the cathedral and get to that pizza parlor across the street before it became too crowded. We followed the group to the largest of the buildings, which, it turned out, was the cathedral. On the outside, all the buildings, including the cathedral, were rather shabby. The original colors had long since faded; here and there rain had worn away large stretches of the cement veneer, exposing old, rough-cut stones probably taken from some ancient Native American temple or pyramid. By any standards, the outside of the cathedral was drab and uninviting. It was a most unlikely place to begin our quest for the Holy Grail.

No sooner had we stepped across the threshold, however, than we both began to feel a mighty presence infecting our unsuspecting hearts and minds. At first, we were so disoriented that we were not sure what it was. We left the group of jabbering tourists and sat quietly on the rough wooden benches that filled the center of the church. It was clear that these had been placed here reluctantly, as if they did not really belong. Of course, the benches were a late addition, for the original church had no seating of any kind. It was a great hall into which the colonists crowded for their worship. The Indians, we learned, did not enter here.

As our eyes became accustomed to the startling interior of the building, we realized what had disoriented us as we entered. All of the garish decoration so typical of Spanish colonial churches had been removed. The building was stark in its simplicity but somehow warm and inviting. Every decoration and appointment inside the huge cathedral was filled with meaning, from the seven hanging lamps around the altar to four more hanging over an ancient open Bible. The whole building seemed to invite us to reflect on the core of Christianity, word and sacrament, and to put aside all other thoughts.

The towering walls were covered with primitive drawings, probably done by some ancient monk who had more fire of devotion than sense of artistry. There was less sense of perspective in the paintings than one sees in elementary school drawings, but there was passion, deep concern, and an effort to tell the story of Mexican Franciscan missionaries in Japan who had been crucified over the hillsides of Nagasaki, 175 years before the United States took its first steps toward nationhood.

The central figure of the story was Mexican-born Felipe de las Casas, a fascinating character by anyone's standards. His devout parents enrolled him in the Franciscan seminary at Puebla when he was only a boy. At eighteen, he had had enough of religious life; he left the seminary, and became a merchant. Filled with a desire for adventure, he set sail for the Philippines to make his fortune. After a few years, he realized that money, power, and fame were not his calling and so decided to reenter the seminary where he would complete his studies. Felipe boarded a ship for Mexico but perverse winds took his ship to Japan instead. There, in Nagasaki (the site where the Americans dropped their second atomic bomb on Japan), he joined other Franciscans and lay Christians in martyrdom in 1597.

As we studied the ancient drawings on the cathedral walls, we wondered where the winds controlling our own lives might take us; we wondered, too, what might be the future of the world we saw around us.[1]

Wandering around the unusual church for some hours, we tried to understand why it was having such a profound effect on us. It seemed timeless: the ancient drawings on the walls, the bold symbols of fire, water, sacrament, and word, the temporary benches that spoke of poverty and incompleteness, the men and women kneeling here and there in an almost mystic state of prayer, and groups of tourists marching through the cathedral with one eye on their watches as they anticipated their next stop on some whirlwind tour of the city. Yet, all this seemed fitting. The old building absorbed us in a mist of piety that would make the most irreverent person thoughtful. For a long time, we sat and pondered, content to be where we were without understanding why we found it exciting and yet deeply peaceful.

The First Beatitude

In this mellow mood, we noticed a large plaque on a wall. It stood alone; there was no other decoration on the walls except the primitive pictures of the Franciscans in Japan. The plaque had no pictures, but only the beatitudes, those short sayings of Jesus that sum up his moral teaching. We glanced at the Spanish and were about to move on when the first beatitude struck us. In a few words something that had troubled us for years suddenly leaped into awful clarity. It read, "Happy are those who have the spirit of the poor....."[2]

We had spent half a lifetime struggling with the more familiar "poor in spirit." We had read the biblical commentaries and the works of the spiritual writers but that first beatitude had always been a tantalizing mystery, especially when we compared these words from Matthew with what was probably an earlier version in Luke where the words "in spirit" are missing. We have known for many years that Jesus tied holiness to poverty in some mysterious way. That is clear enough in the gospels, even when we were determined not to see it. But we have always wondered how you could be poor when you were born into some wealth, given an extensive education, become dependent on clean water and food, insurance and medical attention, warmth in the cold and, more recently, protection against the heat as well.

So much of what we had studied was no more than an attempt to dismiss the awful impact of the words. Somehow we were told that Jesus did not mean what he had said. To be poor in spirit did not mean embracing poverty as a way of life; it did not mean sharing the lives of the poor or renouncing any of our wealth. It meant instead no more than remaining detached from riches while continuing to enjoy them, something we had always wondered about, since living a truly poor life did not seem possible, at least for us.

We had talked with priests and religious who have tried to simplify their own lives by not having maids in order to live more simply, and with couples who had given up big incomes to work among the poor. We ourselves had followed this route, giving what we could to the poor and living as simply as possible. Yet, we had always sensed that this was only part of what that beatitude was trying to teach. We had even wondered whether those of us born into the ease of the First World could ever taste the happiness Jesus promised to the poor.

Now it was clear what we were to do and where our adventure would take us. We had to taste the "spirit of the poor" and to embrace it for ourselves. This was the price of the happiness Jesus promised. The unusual translation made it clear to us; a revelation was beginning to dawn on us. We did not yet understand its full meaning but the direction we had to follow was clear at last.

The spirit of the poor, like the spirit of America or the spirit of the church or the spirit of a baseball team, is not easily defined. It is something you catch, not something you set out to deliberately define and encase in a mental construct. The spirit of a group of people is a combination of many things. It is a way of valuing life, deciding what is important and why. It is a pattern of thought, a way of understanding relationships and things around us. It is a way of expressing love through acts of kindness and generosity. It is a way of refusing to consider some aspects of reality and avoiding them altogether. The spirit of a group is as hard to define as it is hard to avoid. The Spirit of God was so real to Jesus and his followers that it was God. The spirit of the poor, we have discovered, is so real that it is the poor. More about all this later.

Spirituality

We over-theologized Catholics like to call this bundle of attitudes and assumptions a "spirituality," but that is an obscene word. A detached spirituality removes us from the hurly-burly of a real life: its passion, its music, and its excitement. It reduces the core of life to a wispy, gossamer construct without blood or passion. It is an ideal subject for books written by recluses and introverts and read in the main by other equally withdrawn people who believe that only they are really religious. Little wonder that religion has attracted so few vibrant, excited, and happy people.

From the beginning we were determined to avoid that sort of minor heresy. God made us aggressive, outgoing, passionate people and these qualities, as much as any others, were and are the image of God Genesis talked about. God is not a withdrawn introvert, spending time copying manuscripts or anything else. God is always on the move, always creating, not copying, always passionately in love. The Bible never suggests that God is a withdrawn celibate. It does compare God to a passionate lover frustrated by the beloved's lack of response (Hosea 1–3) and as a father who is never quite sure what the children will do next but manages to love them all the same (Luke 10:25–37). And then there was Jesus. He was anything but withdrawn. Ask the scribes and Pharisees about that.

What we were looking for was the spirit of the poor, the spirit of a people caught up in all the excitement of being alive, men and women who feel as well as think, who fall passionately in love and decorate their lives with the world's brightest colors and most tender music, youth who dream, and old women who tend their grandchildren with a hope for their future.

We knew that we were going to have to enter these lives, so different from our own, if they would let us. It would not be enough to give something to the poor, however much they might need. We were going to have to become their friends, their companions, and even their disciples. Whatever knowledge, prestige, and wealth we had accumulated in our half-century of life was, temporarily at least, valueless. We were back at the beginning of life, almost like little children knocking at the door of adulthood begging to be admitted. It was a humbling experience. Yet it was exciting, too, for it was like being born again. Who knew what joy this new life might bring?

We remembered the story of Francis of Assisi who met a leper on the road and threw the unfortunate man a bag of money, all he had. Francis tried to ride away, but could not. In a moment he knew that he had to share the leper's life and learn from him what it was to see the face of God. God has a way of hiding in the most unlikely places. The condition to encounter a revelation is to meet God where God really is.

With New Hearts

We left the cathedral with our hearts and minds bloated by the revelation. We knew how the prophets must have felt and perhaps how Joseph of Nazareth felt after his encounter with the angel in his dream. Like Joseph, we had a new vision of what our life would be, one we had not really asked for. Now we had to do something about it. Joseph's story was especially forceful because he was instructed to take Mary as his wife and form an intimate bond with her, a bond so tender and so all-engulfing that even the authors of the gospels never tried to describe it. This was the kind of bond we knew we had to forge with the poor. How it would happen, we did not know. We did understand that our lives would never be the same again, any more than Joseph's life was after his dream.

In a way, we were like the young man in the *Iron John* stories. We had experienced a mysterious initiation rite whose meaning would become clear only after living it out for years. We were ready for whatever would come our way.

With new eyes we saw the Indians struggling to sell a few souvenirs on the sidewalk by the fortress door. Going in we had felt sorry for them. Coming out we knew that they were going to be our teachers and guides. Everything was new because we were renewed. Like the people in the primitive sketches on the cathedral wall, we were setting out on a journey and now understood where to begin and who would guide us. That we were in our fifties meant little, for our hearts were as young as they had ever been.

Our goal was to discover and embrace the spirit of the poor. Here we would find God and new meaning for our lives. The adventure was in focus; the journey had begun.

—Chapter Two—

Our First Faltering Steps

From our sometimes comical mistakes and false starts we learn how far we are from understanding the spirit of the poor.

The experience at the cathedral burned in our memories. It was like one of those dreams recorded in the Bible, pivotal events which opened a new door in life and set a new and unexpected goal. Carl Jung, the psychoanalyst of dreams, was always interested in a dream that had in it a door to a new room. He saw this as a sign that a new phase was about to open in a person's life. Our moment of intense insight into the spirit of the poor, this flash of understanding, was like one of those dreams. In fact, what we thought was a large plaque on the cathedral wall was in fact a door. We had no doubt that our task was to go through a door into some new life in which we would catch and hold on to the "spirit of the poor," whatever that might be.

Like so many dreams, however, this one soon began to fade. The colors, the certainty, the clarity—all of these—lost some of their luster as we plunged into the task of learning to live in a new environment. The dream was there but it kept going in and out of focus, the way profound revelations do. What we did not realize was that even our mundane concerns about learning to live in this new culture were building up to a stage from which we could step forward, toward our goal.

Humble Beginnings

The first task facing us with some urgency was setting up housekeeping. It sounded simple enough. We had a place to live, a house near downtown Cuernavaca, and Patty could cook. What else was there? The first few months proved there was a great deal more. Each step of the way took us closer to our goal of discovering the spirit of the poor, although we did not realize it at the time. Instead, we lived with frustration, discouragement, and at times a smoldering anger, until we realized how foolish we must seem to others.

We had never admitted how much we were prisoners of our own North American expectations until they clashed with everyday life in Mexico. In fact, we liked to think of ourselves as more flexible and adaptable than most. We had lived in different parts of the United States and adapted well to regional differences. We had raised children with all the reassessment of goals that that implies, and we had changed careers in mid-life. Since we are flexible, we thought adapting to life in the Third World would present no serious problem. That confident belief in our flexibility was shattered the first time we ordered LP gas for our kitchen.

Ordering gas seemed the easiest thing in the world to do. Mexico has a telephone system and even yellow pages in the phone directory. With our halting Spanish we called the gas company. The cheerful voice on the other end told us that they would deliver the gas "tomorrow or the day after."

"What time will that be, in the morning or the afternoon?" Patty innocently asked. The idea of waiting in the house for two days seemed unnecessary. We knew we had to be present when the truck arrived in order to pay in cash. People in Mexico do not use checks the way they do in the U.S., and there is no such thing as credit.

"Tomorrow or the day after," was the only reply.

We were confused but we tried to begin our vigil calmly early the next morning. Each time we heard a heavy truck we rushed to the window, but the day passed without any sign of the gas truck. The next day passed without the gas delivery and so did the next. By this time our composure was beginning to show signs of strain. During the three days of waiting from morning to night we called the gas company repeatedly. The cheerful voice always answered, "Tomorrow or the day after. That's absolutely certain." Our nerves were frayed but we grumbled only to each other, since we did not yet know how to do it in Spanish.

By the second day of our vigil, we ran out of gas, of course, and had to eat in a neighborhood restaurant. Since we were on "gas vigil" though, we could not leave the house together before 7:00 in the evening. Reluctantly, we went our separate ways until finally, on the fourth day, late in the afternoon when we were about to give up hope, an ancient truck appeared. Everyone smiled, the workers because they always smiled, and we because we would have enough gas for six weeks and could once more do something other than wait for the gas truck.

We had learned our first big lesson about life in Mexico. Things are not as simple and uncomplicated as they seem. Without realizing it, we had joined the poor in their endless waiting for almost everything. It was not a pleasant experience, for we were easily frustrated, but, as we later understood, a very important one.

Another experience from those early days was learning to use the toilet. This may sound like "potty training revisited," and it was. Friends told us that Mexican sewerage pipes were unlike those we were used to. At the first sign of overload, they refused to work at all. The only way to avoid problems was to place the used toilet paper in a container next to the toilet and empty the container regularly.

That sounds easy enough but years of disposing of the paper in the toilet is a habit not easily overcome. There is a sickening feeling that comes over you just after you by mistake drop the paper into the water. You pray that this time the sewerage system will forgive you. You push the lever and wait. With one hand on the plunger, you hope a plumber will not be necessary. More impatience on our part, more frustration, and a readiness to believe that we were not as flexible as we had imagined.

And then there was the water. We have been fortunate to have enough water even in the six-month dry season when it never rains at all. Many of our neighbors have to hire a tank truck to deliver water to their homes and many poor families have no water at all. Our problem, as North Americans, was that our bodies would not tolerate the bacteria and amoebas in the local water. Every drop we consumed had to be boiled twenty minutes, then cooled. In the beginning, it seemed like a full-time job. Remembering to use the right water when we brushed our teeth was one of life's challenges. We were easily discouraged by the need to take such excessive precautions; we wondered whether we would ever have time to do anything else but boil and cool water.

Transportation was another problem. Before leaving the United States, we had decided that we would not own a car. This was one of our few good decisions, but it did mean we had to learn how to use the bus system and, with a very limited knowledge of Spanish, this proved quite a challenge. We waited on the wrong street corners, got off at the wrong places, and took the wrong buses. We lived in a kind of fog, always near to frustration. But, with time, this too became an amusing memory.

The gas, the toilet, the water, and the transportation were humiliating experiences. All the time we had planned to spend getting to know the poor, becoming one of them, and helping them was being consumed by these taken-for-granted services. Slowly, we were learning how complicated life can be in Mexico and how frustrating for anyone raised in the U.S. This was our first taste of a kind of oppression born of poverty. It was not the poverty of individuals or even of groups but the poverty of a whole society. We knew the statistics.[1] The annual per capita income in the U.S. is $16,444 while in Mexico the figure is $2082, that Mexico's population had jumped from 10 million in 1900 to over 90 million today, that the U.S. has one telephone for every 1.9 people while Mexico has one for every 8.8 people. Now we were translating those statistics into everyday realities. The small per capita income meant that gas companies have few delivery trucks, cities have inadequate water and sewerage systems, and that buses are old and worn out. The incredible population explosion (900% in less than a century) means that most workers are young, inexperienced, and poorly schooled. The telephone statistics mean that many businesses have no phone at all; even when they do, the employees are using an unfamiliar instrument they may never use at home.

Here we were in the middle of a society that could not deliver safe drinking water, whose telephones did not always work, whose sewage was a serious problem, and whose buses, though many, were poorly marked and would never have been allowed on U.S. streets. There were ways to avoid many of these inconveniences, we learned from our North American friends—hiring a maid, for example—but to do so would have made finding the spirit of the poor more difficult. We decided we had to live as Mexicans did and perhaps then we would take our first halting steps toward our goal.

Looking back on these first months, we laugh at our arrogance. Without realizing it, we expected life to be as it had always been. Like most North Americans, our tolerance for frustration was low. Adapting to a very different way of life consumed our days but began to teach us that the beginning of discovering the spirit of the poor was to experience their frustrations in a society that knows only poverty.

In the midst of these frustrations that seem so minor now but were major events in those early days, we never lost sight of that goal we set for ourselves in the cathedral. We wanted to be about the work of finding the spirit of the poor and embracing it. What we did not realize was that these frustrations were preparing us for the task ahead. If the spirit of the poor means anything it means practicing patience in the face of life's outrages.

Making Our Beginning

We had come to Mexico as freelancers with no obligation to any group. This gave us freedom, but with that freedom came a lack of security. No one had mapped out for us a program of work, a schedule to follow. In the beginning, we were not sure that anyone wanted our help.

The year before we left for Mexico we had often visited our daughter who was training (at Maryknoll, New York) to be a lay missioner. We were interested in learning what she learned because our adventure and hers were to be very much alike. One theme we heard repeatedly at Maryknoll was that the first year in a foreign land would be unsettling and discouraging. They warned the young missionaries that they would make many false starts, experience failure, and even wonder why they had left home at all.

We listened to this with that superior smirk born of middle age and complete inexperience. Our age convinced us that these were problems for the young, kids our daughter's age, and not for us. After all, we were not going to make any false starts—we had a lifetime's experience to guide us. We expected no failure, for failure was a thing of our past and we rarely indulged in crying over spilled milk. These were the problems of youth, we were quite sure. We could not imagine ourselves making a series of false starts and falling victim to discouragement after all we had been through to arrange our move to Mexico.

Despite the fact that we had never lived abroad, we were confident that life in one country was bound to be pretty much the same as in another. Our trips as tourists had never left us troubled or discouraged. The little problems the older missionaries enumerated for our daughter would, we were sure, never bother us. We would never admit that we might be making many false starts.

Buoyed up with this unreal confidence, we were ready to discover the spirit of the poor. We made our plans without a moment's hesitation. We knew where we were going and we would get there. Only our lack of Spanish stood in our way and that handicap would, we were sure, be overcome in a few months. Hadn't we seen the ads that promised we could speak Spanish like a diplomat in just a few weeks?

Well, the old saying is still true, "Pride goes before the fall." And fall we did, not once but more times than we can now count. Everything the old missionaries had told our daughter at Maryknoll was true, true in spades for us who had ventured out alone to live in a very different land.

Our First Failure

We had visited Cuernavaca many times before coming to live here and had made promising contacts with men and women who were working with the poor. Three different groups had encouraged us to work with them. Because all three of these programs were so interesting and obviously anchored in the same kind of beliefs we brought with us, we wanted to help all of them.

One group, an ecumenical retreat center, brought North Americans to Mexico to expose them to the lives and problems of the poor in the Third World. Once exposed to these problems and aware that the First World was the cause of so many of them, the hope was that these retreatants would go home, share their experiences, and work to change things in their own communities. That was the theory of "reverse mission," and it made sense to us. We made one of these retreats and were convinced that they were worthwhile. We volunteered to be a part of the staff and worked with them for more than six months.

At the time this seemed like a good idea; we could use many of our educational and management skills and could speak English most of the time. The program called for men and women who believed in liberation, justice, and the kingdom of God. These were our beliefs, too, so we were ready to go. Without realizing it, however, we were looking for an easy way to discover the spirit of the poor, a way that did not demand that we share our lives with them. Working at this retreat center was good work, important work perhaps, but we soon learned that it would not take us toward our goal.

Our first sign that this was the wrong place for us was the stress we discovered within the staff. In fact, it seemed that more of our energy went into staff struggles than into the retreat experiences themselves. The whole situation had a familiar ring: individualism, contentiousness, and a constant struggle in the pecking order. It was so like the U.S. we began to wonder if this mysterious spirit of the poor we had come to find was here at all. What confused us was that all staff members professed a belief in human liberation and the coming of the kingdom of God on earth. This was what we also believed.

During a staff training session, we studied a pamphlet called *The Road to Damascus*[2] written by a group of Third World Christians from seven different countries. The booklet carefully detailed their understanding of Christianity in today's world. It was a radical statement of Third World theology which made great sense to us but, we quickly learned, not to everyone.

Almost all those who studied this document with us were obviously uncomfortable. One young man wondered aloud if this was some new "church party line" that everyone was being forced to follow. He seemed to be reflecting on his old catechism days and feared that this new thought was merely replacing an older model of understanding Jesus. He did not want one set of dogmas to replace another. As we came to know him better, we understood that he was deeply troubled by anything that called into question the role of the U.S. government in world affairs. His parents— good, kind people—among many others, supported the government. He seemed to equate people who supported the government with what it did. Religion, he felt, had no place in politics.

Unfortunately, contemporary Latin American theology will not condone separating religion from political life. When we read passages like this one, the young man felt that his country and his religion were in question:

> Christian faith has now been introduced into political conflict. Both oppressor and oppressed seek religious legitimation. Both sides invoke the name of God and of Jesus Christ, and Christians are found on both sides of the political conflict in most of our seven countries.
>
> Nor does the matter end there. The political conflict has now entered into the churches. The church itself has become a site of struggle. Some sectors of the church align themselves with the status quo and defend it passionately, while others align themselves with the oppressed and struggle for change. There are yet others who claim to be neutral. In fact, neutrality plays into the hands of those in power because it enables them to continue and to discredit the Christians who oppose them. Neutrality is an indirect way of supporting the status quo.[3]

This young man's feelings were not unique. We discovered many people who made the retreats held similar beliefs. They could not understand how the U.S. government could be at fault when so many kind, decent people supported it. The very mention of the conflict that exists between the rich and the poor sent many of these people into terrible fits of anger or depression. These were good people who wanted to help the poor but who bridled at the mention of the possibility that they were called to change their lifestyles and become poor themselves.

These were real problems, ones worthy of hard work, but they were not leading us to the spirit of the poor. Instead, they were focusing our attention on the problems of the rich and powerful, people so much like us who lived in the First World. We began to understand that the poor people of the Third World would have to force a change and no amount of talking with First World people would prepare them for the changes the poor would inevitably demand. The situation was very much like the Civil Rights struggle of the 1960s in the southern United States. Only when the oppressed black people demanded a change did a change come. The lever for change in Latin America had to be manipulated by the poor. The Third World statement we were studying went on to say:

> We must take seriously Jesus' accusation of hypocrisy. We cannot sit on the fence and profess neutrality while people are being persecuted, exploited and killed. We cannot remain silent because we fear the authorities and do not want to rock the boat. Jesus calls all hypocrites to conversion.[4]

These were strong words, upsetting words for those who read them. In our group of staff members, there were many different reactions. One man was concerned that these ideas were presented as true rather than as one possible opinion. His way of neutralizing the fire of the document was to make it relative. For him and others like him, theological truth was a rare commodity; most statements were no more than the opinions of those who wrote them.

Other staff members were more attuned to the document; they believed in justice, but their sense of justice was often no more than a discomfort with the fact that people in the First World had far more than those in the Third. They wanted to force the rich to give to the poor so that in the end everyone would have an equal amount of the world's goods. This was an admirable stance but one that centered its focus on the First World and its selfishness and did not question whether the poor really wanted this kind of justice. Perhaps they did. We didn't know though, because we had not yet found the spirit of the poor.

This experience at the retreat center was helpful; it highlighted the differences between what most North American church people believe and what Third World theologians are saying. The whole experience reminded us of a passage from a talk delivered in 1962 by the Jesuit theologian, Juan Luis Segundo.

We have lost the force of early Christians. Our words do not express Christianity, but merely express the fact that our social structures have Christian trimmings. And in Latin America, the very words we use in evangelization have been corrupted; try to speak of charity, poverty or the afterlife, and you will be told, "Go away, we know all about your Christianity."

Unfortunately they do know. Every word of the Christian message has been used to support the status quo of Christendom but Christianity itself has been compromised by this attempt to maintain control of the masses, preserving conservatism. All this is justified on the basis that without this economic power and social influence it would be impossible to preach Christianity to the masses but this only means that it would be impossible to maintain the social machine as a "machine to make Christians."[5]

Segundo's words were harsh and the words of the Third World Christians in *The Road to Damascus* were harsher yet. We could understand why so many North Americans had trouble with them. Yet, these words were the voice of the poor and it was to the poor we had come. It was time to admit that we had made a false start in trying to work at the retreat center where thoughts and attitudes were, when all was said and done, little different from those we had left behind in the First World.

We understood that this was not the right place for us to begin our search. Sadly we concluded that these were motivated people but their concerns were not ours. Something in our hearts resonated to the challenges of the Third World theologians. Even if we were at times afraid where this might lead, we had to venture forth. We had to move on, but where we were not sure. This was the first false start we had been warned about but refused to heed.

Our Second Try

Never easily discouraged, we began to devote more and more time to another group of people, the Latin Americans who worked in the Popular Movement. They were good people who tried to enable the poor to take charge of their own lives through leadership training, building up local centers, and initiating self-help projects. We liked what they were doing and we volunteered to help.

We found ideological compatibility with them. They could easily have written the pamphlet that had caused so much trouble at the retreat center. They believed that the poor had to take the initiative if meaningful social change was to take place. The more we were with these people, the more we appreciated the profound difference between the North Americans at the retreat center and these educated Latin Americans. We thought we had found a home.

As the weeks turned into months, we both began to feel compromised and uncomfortable without knowing why. One evening at a party for the staff workers, the reason dawned on us: There were no poor people present. These motivated men and women saw themselves as helpers of the poor, but not as part of their community. Their working hours were spent helping the poor— but their recreation was taken apart from them. They had created a difference—and a distance—between themselves and the poor.

About this time, we were reading more and more about the incarnation. From childhood we had professed and believed that God became one of us. But did we really understand this? The key to understanding it was God's closeness to us, intimacy with the human race. As a married couple deeply in love with each other, this made sense. The more passionately you love, the more time you want to spend with your beloved, the more you want to be identified with him or her. Our experience as man and woman and as father and mother had taught us that true love demands closeness, intimacy, and a complete sharing of life. In a family, that intimacy is so total that there is no place for playing roles or attempting to live separate lives. This desire for intimacy with the poor was what we found lacking among our dedicated friends. They wanted to do good things for the poor, but did not take concrete steps to be truly one of them.

The model they used was that of an agency. We believed that the family was the model that best reflected the truth of the incarnation. As husband and wife we had had experiences that gave us a profound insight into God. We were learning wonderful techniques for community organization, important social theory, and significant insights into the minds of educated Latin Americans. Yet, what was missing was an opportunity to learn the spirit of the poor directly—and to treasure it. It was time to move on while keeping our relationship to the Popular Movement intact. This, too, was another false start.

Our Third Try

The third group we were aware of was six Mexican Benedictine Sisters who lived in La Nopalera, one of Cuernavaca's poorest slums. They lived a poor lifestyle and shared the daily lives of the poor around them. Since there were no priests in this huge area of 85,000 people, the sisters acted as pastors of five chapels, leading prayer services, preparing people for the sacraments, and most important, forming small communities to reflect on the meaning of the gospel in their daily lives. The sisters were our models. We decided to attend services each Sunday and if possible to become part of their parish. We never expected this experience to be our most profound and intense introduction to the spirit of the poor.

It was here that we caught our best insight into what it means to be poor. In this context we began to taste the spirit of the poor, to become friends with them, to understand their joys and their suffering, and to be accepted into their community not as people who came with money or ideas to help them, but simply to be one of them, to be their friends.

Slowly, over a period of several months, we began to understand that our other involvements were standing in the way of our most important goal, to understand the spirit of the poor. We were faced with a dilemma, for these other projects were good works, too, and provided us with many comforts, speaking English to interested people, access to a swimming pool during the interminable dry season, contact with many interesting academics, easy check-cashing arrangements, and the like. Yet, our need to devote ourselves full time to living the life of the poor became stronger and stronger as the months passed.

We knew that the translation of the beatitude so often rendered, "Happy are the pure of heart," was inadequate because it made people think of sexual purity and this was not the real meaning of the beatitude. Instead, it talks of one's overall commitment to the Lord and might better be translated, "Happy are the single-minded." It was time we put this beatitude into practice.

Our minds and hearts were cluttered by demands that pulled us in different directions. We were at a point in life much like that of the rich young man in the gospel whom Jesus invited to sell what he owned, give it to the poor, and follow him. If Jesus was to be found among the poor—and we firmly believed he was—then the poor had to claim first place in our lives. Painfully, we left other involvements, good works, and interesting challenges behind and went stumbling along after Jesus in the poor.

In these first months in Cuernavaca, we had begun to question our traditional Christian piety, to wonder if the gospel as we had received it had not been tamed or domesticated over the centuries. Had Jesus said something much more disconcerting and challenging than we had ever imagined? Was it his uncompromisingly radical message that led to his crucifixion? Would our following this kind of leadership lead us to something we did not expect?

These were unsettling questions, ones we were tempted not to think too much about. At this moment in our lives, our task was to seize the opportunity at hand. Later we would see where this radical Jesus might lead us. For now, it was enough to give up what we had and to follow him.

Making Sense of Our Experiences

We had now met and worked with three different groups of people. Two of them we left behind in our search for a deeper understanding of the spirit of the poor. We were not completely sure why we felt compelled to do this and longed for an insight into what was happening so rapidly in our lives.

About this time we began to reflect on information we had stumbled upon a few years earlier: the dramatic difference among popular lifestyles and value systems in the United States. Researchers at Stanford Research Institute in California had identified nine distinct lifestyles, each with its own set of values, goals, and expectations. This information guided advertising firms in finding the right target for their ads. The ideas seemed valid, for the United States at least, and we wondered if it would help us understand why we had had to leave two of the first three groups with whom we tried to work and why we felt so comfortable with the third. Even though the research findings appeared coldly scientific, we suspected that it might have a lot to offer us in our search to find the spirit of the poor.[6]

This schema divides the U.S. population into three very diverse classes called the Cultural Center, the Cultural Left, and the Cultural Right. These names have nothing to do with political or religious beliefs but instead stand for three different subcultures in the U.S., each with its own set of values and life expectations.

The first, which Tex Sample calls the Cultural Middle, is composed of those who are driven by the work ethic and the desire to achieve. The three subdivisions of this Cultural Middle are: those who achieve successfully, those who merely strive to be successful and may one day reach their goal, and those who work hard but will never be successful and they know it. Most rich and middle-class people fall into this group of the Cultural Middle. The suburban executive who spends long days at the office and through great effort rises from rags to riches is the archtypical group member. He realizes that his job may take him and his family to different cities during his lifetime but that is acceptable for he is competing to get to the top and whatever that takes is worthwhile. He and his family live well, accept the values of the community, and even make donations to help the less fortunate. Yet, the center of their lives is his drive toward success.

Of this group, Sample writes:

> People who pursue careers carry the dominant, established
> ways of doing things in U.S. society. They embody the cul-
> ture at its idealized "best." Actively involved in the search
> for success, achievement, and the state of being Number
> One, they have extraordinary affirmation of their effort at
> every hand.[7]

The second group, the Cultural Left, are those who, like the
first group, are independent of any special location but who have
consciously rejected personal achievement in favor of self-
fulfillment. Included here are those whose lives are spent searching for every new experience, and those who have a strong social,
but not personal, morality. Many of these people are young, well-
educated, and have refused to compete for the riches offered to
those who conform successfully to the norms of the business community and instead have gone to Vermont to raise goats, ski, join
the peace movement, and care for the environment. They are often called non-conformist but they do conform to an inner desire
for self-fulfillment rather than personal achievement.

The third group, the Cultural Right, are those whose lives are
circumscribed by the place in which they live. They are the men
and women who remain in the town or neighborhood of their
birth, go into a local business, marry someone from the old neighborhood, and live there happily ever after. Among them are the
respectable locals, those who imitate them but never achieve re-
spectability, and the desperately poor. These local people cannot
understand either the highly competitive achiever of the Cultural
Middle or the non-conformist on the Cultural Left. The man or
woman in the Cultural Right wonders aloud whether the others
are really Christian or American.

We asked ourselves how this schema might apply to the Mexico we were coming to understand and to the three groups we had
met and worked with: the North Americans at the retreat center,

the group who worked in the Popular Movement, and the poor at La Nopalera.

The Retreat Center

The Cultural Center model provided an easy key to help us understand our North American friends at the retreat center. They were proud of their achievements; they prized the hard work that had gone into attaining them. They were typical North American achievers. We met this same kind of person in other North American institutions in Cuernavaca and noticed their tendency to remain aloof from the local culture that presented a very different set of values and expectations.

When Latin American theologians suggested that what they had achieved was meaningless and perhaps even evil, or that the U.S. government was pursuing a policy inimical to the gospel, many of them bridled at the suggestion and became defensive. Not to work hard, not to achieve, not to run successful programs was somehow un-Christian, slothful, and certainly un-American, or so it seemed to them after spending a lifetime in a lifestyle dominated by achievement.

We realized that we had shared much of that lifestyle but were trying to break out of it and embrace something different and totally new for us. It made sense, then, to leave this group as we sought to taste the spirit of the poor. Since the findings of the Stanford Research Institute had helped us understand one group, we wondered what it would have to say about the other two.

The Popular Movement

The difference between the Popular Movement people who worked with the poor, and the poor themselves was partly economic. The group who worked with the poor were part of the middle class. But was there a more profound difference between these two groups, something deeper than the amount of money they had?

From Dr. Ross Gandy of the Autonomous University in Mexico

City we learned that 70% of Mexicans live outside the consumer economy and are deemed fortunate when they have a place to live and enough to eat. This majority of Mexicans seemed to fit easily into the Cultural Right of the VALS research, those circumscribed by the place and circumstances of their lives. These are the poor of Mexico.

On the other hand, a tiny percentage of Mexicans are obscenely wealthy and a relatively small middle class has developed since the 1950s whose values ape those of the wealthy. We wondered how the middle class compared to similar groups in the U.S., whether they were moved by a desire for personal achievement or perhaps were more like the mostly younger Americans who did not desire to achieve but only to experience an inner sense of self-fulfillment.

Through reading and personal contact we began to understand that the rich in Mexico and the middle class who imitate them were not interested in the kind of personal achievement so important in the U.S. They were not infected by the work ethic. In fact, many did not work at all. They cultivated relationships and spent their time in every imaginable form of recreation. Many of the middle class did work hard but only to achieve the goal of not working and having the time to cultivate relationships and to engage in diverse forms of recreation.

It was clear that the self-fulfillment ethic, new in the U.S., was the dominant goal among the rich and middle class in Mexico and had been for centuries. Their sense of personal success was defined in terms of tending relationships and having time for recreation, not what they had achieved by their own efforts. Work, both physical and mental, was something to be delegated to servants. They were more like those who have dropped out of the system in the U.S. (for example, the men and women, mostly young, who have gone to Vermont to ski and raise goats) than like their success-driven parents who feel they must work even though they have no need for more money.

There were, of course, exceptions: Mexicans of all classes who were more like North Americans than like their own compatriots. This was especially true among the younger, middle-class Mexicans who had been educated in the U.S. Yet, with this said, it was true that most middle-class Mexicans hoped to become men and women of leisure and to the degree possible practice that lifestyle now. Thus, the hard-driving efficiency so common in the U.S. was left to the poor who could never hope to share in the lifestyles of the rich or even the middle class. The poor worked hard because they had to.

The reason for this difference between Mexicans and North Americans may have its roots in colonial days. Spain denied all authority and responsibility for governing Mexico to anyone not born in the mother country. A very small class of native-born Spaniards exercised all authority in the country. Those born in Mexico, no matter how talented or how wealthy, were wards of the state and expected to do nothing. That tradition has endured.

We could now grasp why middle-class Mexicans from the Popular Movement, the second group we had left behind in our search, did their work with so little apparent drive. Like people of their class and educational background, they enjoyed cultivating relationships among themselves, talking about and analyzing the problems of poverty, and planning parties and other recreational events for the staff under the rubric of building community. To do otherwise for them was somehow un-Christian, rigid, and certainly un-Mexican. Many felt that these values made them more compatible with the demands of the gospel and the insights of the Latin American theologians.

The Poor

We now felt we understood the two groups we had left behind in our journey, the North Americans at the retreat center and the middle-class Mexicans who worked with the poor. That left us with the poor themselves, seven out of ten people in Mexico. They worked harder than most people did in the U.S. They labored from dawn to well after sunset, had almost no protection against illness and injury, had few tools to ease their labor, and were rewarded by a wage so meager that it barely sustained their lives and those of their families. Were they, however, driven by the work ethic or by absolute necessity? They expected to work hard and never shirked responsibility. Many took great pleasure in the achievements of their trade and enjoyed repairing complex machinery. Yet, this work was not an end in itself or a sign of their success. They enjoyed working but also enjoyed cultivating relationships and what little recreation came their way. Of all the classes of people we met, American or Mexican, the poor seemed to be the most balanced and perhaps the happiest. This should not have surprised us in view of Jesus' teaching, but it did.

Like poorer North Americans, they were bound to the place in which they were born by deep psychological ties. Even though they had to leave the rural areas to find work, they talked longingly of their *tierra*, their land, their place in the universe. This made creating a new community of exiles in places like La Nopalera a profound challenge.

Unlike poorer North Americans, these men and women felt no sense of personal failure in being poor. They realized it was the economic system, not their own lack of hard work, that made them poor. Poverty like intelligence was an accident of birth. This attitude relieved them of the terrible guilt that American poor carry and left them free to enjoy what little they had.

Mexican Lifestyles

The lifestyles of Mexico were different from those we in the United States cultivated. There was no clear place for the achiever, the efficient, hard-driving Horatio Alger. The North American Cultural Center lifestyle was beginning to invade but it was still present in only a small minority. Most Mexicans believed that recreation and personal relationships were more important than what North Americans considered important. Alan Riding, perhaps the most outstanding analyst of things Mexican, writes:

Mexico is today preparing for the twenty-first century without having dealt with the legacy of the sixteenth century. The problems of under-development are being compounded by over-development, hopeless poverty is coinciding with excessive growth, the weight of the past is pulling against the magnet of the future. More complex than rich versus poor, urban versus rural or Right versus Left, the dilemma touches on the fundamental issue of Mexico's profile as a nation. A new head has been transplanted onto an old body—a Westernized, restless, individualistic and materialistic minority imposed on an Oriental, conformist, communitarian and traditional majority—and the relationship is uncomfortable.[8]

Looking Inward

When we thought about ourselves, we knew we were part of the Cultural Middle, like most North Americans. We had unconsciously defined our success in terms of books written, the degrees attained, real estate owned, and the business balance sheet. Yet, we had always been uncomfortable with these values because the gospel seemed to be saying something different about success. As we studied the various lifestyles outlined in the VALS research, we failed to find one that was completely comfortable for us. Perhaps, we prayed, the life of the Mexican poor might open to us yet another way of living that embodied the ideal we had come to Mexico to find. We knew this was necessary if we were ever to meet God face to face in the lives of the poor.

—Chapter Three—

The Pearl of Great Price

We make our first friends at La Nopalera and begin to understand the people's attitudes toward poverty, generosity, and children.

The Pearl

There is nothing more fascinating than a seminal insight, a thought that lights up your mind in a momentary flash of excitement. When we stumble upon one, digest it, test it, and integrate it into our own synthesis of life, we think, "How utterly simple and obviously true this insight is. How could we have missed it? Or forgotten it? Or only half-noticed it? As Jesus said in one of his parables, 'This is the pearl of great price.'"

Our pearl was very simple. In order to find and embrace the spirit of the poor, we had to give up all distractions and plunge headlong into their everyday lives. It was not enough to talk about poverty or to plan programs to obliterate it or even to be friends with those who want to help the poor. What we needed to do was to stand side by side with the poorest of the poor, to walk in their shoes, and to live their lives if we were ever to understand their spirit.

With this pearl in our pockets, La Nopalera, the poor neighborhood where we had already begun to attend Mass on Sunday, became the center of our lives. This was to be our way of discovering the spirit of the poor. We were convinced that we were at last on the right track.

La Nopalera

In 1973, a radical young activist, Florencio Medrano, appeared on the Cuernavaca scene. He was fresh from a study of peasant life in Mao's China where he had witnessed poor people's take-overs of unused land. Clandestinely he organized a group of five thousand landless poor who in a single night occupied a tract of unused land owned by the son of a former governor of the state. The land was an arid tract in which nothing grew except nopales, edible cactus plants. There the poor set up their tar-paper shacks, carried water from a pitiful stream in the middle of the area and began to build a new city, a city of the poor.

Almost as soon as the occupation occurred, the government began to move against it. They hoped to discourage the settlers without a massive slaughter. For seven years, the army ruled the area with an iron fist. Many of the people's leaders were imprisoned and tortured. A few, including Medrano, were assassinated or "disappeared." Today, the people quip about those terrible days of martial law, saying that the army left only when half its soldiers had married the young women of the community.

Under Medrano's leadership, the settlement was organized into neighborhood cells; these determined the rules for the community. Selling liquor, for example, was not allowed and any man who beat his wife was expelled. The settlement grew steadily and its success inspired imitation in Cuernavaca and in other parts of Mexico.

Today there are 85,000 people living in the area. Many of the tar-paper shacks have been replaced by small concrete homes, usually two or three rooms in which eight or ten people live. Reluctantly, the municipal government of nearby Temixco drilled a water well and provided sewers for those located in the center of the settlement. The power company added lights and, a few years ago, part of the area was declared an official *colonia*, or barrio, with its own political leaders. The government then added schools; soon small businesses began to spring up to provide food and some elementary services for the people.

A central figure during these days of oppression was the now retired bishop of Cuernavaca, Don Sergio Mendez Arceo, often called the "red" bishop of Latin America. He distributed Bibles to the people, helped them organize into base communities, and supported them when they decided to do something about their powerless situation. He stood with the people of La Nopalera during their darkest days and even spent his Sunday afternoons doing manual labor on their primitive public works projects.

In 1983, Don Sergio persuaded a group of Mexican Benedictine Sisters to work in the colonia. These sisters were accustomed to working with the poor, especially in schools. Their work here, however, was to be different; since no priest was available or would come to live here, the sisters would be the pastors of the whole settlement. The sisters now have five chapels where they lead services each Sunday. They have built up a network of over 40 base communities. Two former superiors of the congregation work among the people.

The people who live in the area are what Latin American theologians call the marginalized poor, those who live on the outskirts of modern life with no power to influence its ebb and flow. Many, especially the elderly, have no source of income and subsist on the generosity of their neighbors. Some men have found jobs in Cuernavaca doing manual labor where the prevailing wage is about $3.50 (U.S.) a day. A skilled tradesperson makes twice that, about the same as a college-graduate accountant. Many others have had to travel to the United States to work in the fields to send money back to their families. Few women are able to work since many neither read nor write and live an hour by bus from Cuernavaca where most jobs would pay little more than their daily bus fare.

The arid wasteland now is filled with families. The dirt streets echo with the games of countless children. The schools, while incredibly poor by North American standards, are functioning. Water reaches the majority of homes every second day, although many have to rely on water trucks to deliver water to open barrels. Most homes have electricity even though the lines are hung on sticks driven into the ground to carry them. Poverty exists here, but the cloud of outright physical oppression has lifted somewhat and in its place is a gentle cloud of hope.

The people are, by and large, refugees from failed agriculture in neighboring rural states. Most of them are pure Native American, who have lived a communal life for many generations in tiny pueblos where Spanish civilization had little impact. Few read or write, and some speak an indigenous language, not Spanish. Some have never before owned property in their own names and are unfamiliar with money and the modern monetary system.

This is the poor neighborhood in which we wanted to be accepted. We were not sure how to become a part of the community, so we simply wandered about greeting everyone and smiling even when we could not speak or understand much Spanish. We had read about the ideal of inserting oneself into a community. What we read, however, was high on theory and low on practical advice on how to achieve that goal. Because we knew no other way, we decided that we would make ourselves visible, speak to everyone, and hope that something good would happen.

Attending Church

La Nopalera's little chapel breathes poverty. It is rudely constructed of every kind of mismatched local stone with a roof that leaks in at least fifty places. The floors are rough concrete and only some of the window spaces are filled with a cheap colored glass. Because the chapel is in use all week long for every kind of gathering, here and there on the white-washed walls are maps, notices of future meetings, and the notes from past ones. Only a profusion of brightly colored flowers in plastic pails relieves the monotony of the grinding poverty.

At 5:30 each Sunday afternoon we gather for worship, sitting on ancient pews scavenged from the Cuernavaca cathedral, sagging benches, and rickety chairs of various colors. The place is filled with children, teenagers, tired-looking parents, and the placidly beautiful *viejitos*, the old people whom everyone loves. Amid the dust, heat, and confusion, dogs and sometimes chickens play. Birds fly overhead through the open doors and windows, and children return time and again to wash their sweaty faces in the large holy water and baptismal font.

Three Sundays out of four there is no priest present, so one of the sisters leads the service. People come to the church in their pitiful Sunday-best with safety pins and mismatched thread holding their clothes together. Shoeless children are everywhere.

Those who can read serve as lectors and their preparation is obvious as they proclaim the most difficult passages without hesitation. Everyone, even the children, participates in the dialogue homily and the singing while one of the older people distributes Communion. Everyone has a role and fulfills it with dignity and pride.

It was at one of the first celebrations we attended at La Nopalera that we stumbled across Song Number 252 in the hymnal. We recognized it as our traditional "Lord, have mercy" and expected it would merely repeat the ancient text. Instead its lyrics were very different and arresting. Something made us linger to translate this very unusual text.

> *Cristo, Cristo Jesus, identifícate con nosotros.*
> *Señor, Señor mi Dios, identifícate con nosotros.*
> *Cristo, Cristo Jesus SOLIDARIZATE,*
> *no con la clase opresora*
> *que exprime y devora a la comunidad*
> *sino con el oprimido,*
> *con el pueblo mio sediento de paz.*[1]

Our Spanish was still elementary but right away we picked up obvious words: identify, God, Christ, solidarity, oppressive class, devour, community, and peace. "What is this all about?" we asked each other. Perhaps we might not have persisted if we hadn't seen *Solidarizate* in capital letters. Slowly, like drawing a picture, the message came through, and we were thrilled with what we had found.

> Christ, Christ Jesus, identify with us.
> Lord, Lord my God, identify with us.
> Christ, Christ Jesus, stand together,
> not with the oppressor class
> that exhausts and devours the community,
> but with the oppressed,
> with my people thirsting for peace.

After Mass our questions flew back and forth, honing in on the way Jesus chose to stand in solidarity with the poor. He came among us and lived as a poor man; that we knew. Yet, we had never thought of Jesus standing boldly in solidarity with the poor. When we began to think of him that way, we remembered that he was always loyal to the poor of his own day and often confronted the rich and powerful on behalf of the poor. We wondered why Jesus had done that, why he had made this solidarity so central to his ministry.

Hesitantly Bill said, "It's easier to answer that question since we've been coming to La Nopalera. I've come to believe that the poor are truly God's special children. Jesus must have seen what we see, that the poor were suffering at the hands of the rich and powerful. Then he did what his perfect love demanded—he identified with the poor, became one with them. I think we're going to discover other reasons why God chose to send his son to save the world as a poor man. Each day I feel we're coming closer to understanding this."

Patty remembered the quotation (Luke 4:18):

The Spirit of the Lord is upon me. He has anointed me to
bring good news to the poor, to proclaim liberty to captives
and to give new sight to the blind; to free the oppressed and
announce the Lord's year of mercy.

"There it is," Bill replied. "'He has anointed me to bring good
news to the poor....' There are several other places in the gospel
where Jesus speaks of his mission to preach the good news to the
poor."

"And," Patty added, "'Happy are those who have the spirit of
the poor, for theirs is the kingdom of heaven' (Matthew 5:3). "Has
God called us to become in some small way incarnated among the
poor, and for basically the same reasons he sent Jesus to live, die,
and rise to new life among them? Even saying such a thing seems
almost sacrilegious and certainly beyond my own capabilities but
I think we're on to something....Does that sound completely cra-
zy?"

"No, it doesn't," Bill replied. "We need much more time and
experience to know what's really happening. I think we have
stumbled on a model that will be very helpful as we try to stand
by the poor and oppressed. We don't yet understand much but
we can stand and smile and wait. For us, at this point, that will
have to be our solidarity."

A New Beginning

The people of La Nopalera were shy, perhaps a result of the years
of military oppression. They were always polite and never failed
to return our greetings but seldom stopped to talk to us. Each
Sunday we walked the streets in search of a real encounter with
someone other than the sisters, anyone at all.

The moment finally came when ten-year-old Aurelia began to
talk with us on the street near the church. She was a bright-eyed,
slightly chubby girl who would squint up at us in the bright Mexican sun and say "Aurelia, Aurelia" as we tried to understand her
name. She took our hands and walked with us up and down the

street talking animatedly. We understood little of what she said but at last we had what we so desperately wanted, our first friend in La Nopalera. The long wait was ending. We sensed that our patience was soon to be rewarded.

Aurelia often called other children to meet us. She introduced at least ten different children as her *primas*, or cousins. We have never sorted out who is really related to whom since many families take in orphaned children when their parents die. What mattered to Aurelia was not the correct expression of blood ties but the unspoken assumption that cousins care about one another. At last, we were beginning to feel accepted by the children and knew the rest would come in time.

Aurelia did more than introduce us to children during those tentative days. She took us to her mother, Petra, a forceful community leader who reminded us of Deborah or one of the other heroes of the Hebrew Scriptures. Her brown skin and almost chiseled features recalled an ancient Aztec queen. The light in her eyes and her ready smile told us that this woman believed in her own dignity; she had a way of conferring her quiet strength on others. In an instant we knew we were in the presence of a leader. In fact, she and her husband, Eduardo, were the leaders of the local PRD, the Revolutionary Democratic Party, a national political opposition-party active in the colonia. This party and a few others were the focus of a challenge to the Mexican establishment that has treated the poor so shabbily for almost five hundred years.

With Petra, we managed to talk about the United States and its treatment of its own poor. We told her about the blacks, the Native Americans, and the Hispanics in the U.S. and their struggle for equality. Petra listened to our stumbling Spanish and then sagely remarked, "Governments are always the same. They do the work of the rich and care little about the poor. It is the same in your country as in ours." With that, we knew we had been accepted. Petra had watched us arrive on the bus each day and wander about the colonia. She sensed that we were not rich and so were not the enemy.

Another day Aurelia took us to a small house with a large opening overhung with a canopy of torn striped towels. Inside the window, protected from the sun by the towels, were a few cheap pieces of candy for sale. Aurelia and the ever-present cousins wanted us to meet the ancient woman who sat in the semi-darkness behind the candy in her tiny kitchen. She was, they insisted, their *abuelita*, or grandmother. Just whose great-grandmother she is has never become completely clear. Exact relationships are not important in La Nopalera, since all grandmothers (and great-grandmothers) are women who care about all the children.

The old woman, a peasant from the nearby State of Mexico, was called Chonita. With a large toothless smile and eyes that glistened with hidden merriment, she welcomed us and immediately offered us some candy. Her clothing was tattered and worn but like other Mexicans she was striking in her cleanliness. The blue flowers in the material of her dress had faded into the background and a large safety pin gathered her dress at the neck. With an inquisitive smile, she asked where we came from and why we were in La Nopalera so often. It was obvious that she had been watching us walk up and down the street and had wanted to meet us but was too shy to make the first move.

Chonita welcomed our questions, too. We learned that she remembered the Mexican Revolution of 1910-1920; this made her around 90 years of age. She told us about the early days of La Nopalera, the martial law, the lack of water, and the persecutions. Through all her stories she never failed to smile. At 88, as we later learned, she sits selling her candy seven days a week, morning until late evening, hobbling around on her almost immobilized legs.

After our first meeting, we stopped to chat with Chonita whenever we came to La Nopalera; this became a ritual we looked forward to. As we left in the evenings, we told her what we had done that day and explained when we would return. One day, because we had an emergency in Cuernavaca, we did not come to

La Nopalera and by the next day, when we arrived, Chonita was very anxious about what had happened to us. Her worst fear, about which she often needs reassurance, is that we will return to the United States like the other *gringos* we introduce her to from time to time when they are visiting.

Chonita and Petra were our first adult friends besides the sisters. We could feel that the barriers of shyness were breaking down and that we were slowly sliding into the warp and woof of La Nopalera's life as we increased the number of our visits to the colonia.

Each time we arrived at La Nopalera we knew we were being watched—by a little two year old whose mother owned a small fruit stand next to the bus stop. Because the little girl and her mother were very shy, it took several months before the mother, Dona Juana, did more than return our greeting. After months of our coming and going, Dona Juana volunteered that the toddler's name was Rico and tried to pull her from her hiding place to shake hands with us. Rico, with her thin black hair and striking Native American features, was having no part of that and ran through the door-curtain into the house.

We kept making overtures of friendship as we got on and off the bus until one day Dona Juana summoned up the courage to tell us what Rico was doing. "Rico stands in the doorway every day waiting for you to arrive. She looks at each bus that passes and when she spots you, Patty, she screams, *"Mia ginga, mia ginga."*

We laughed with Dona Juana and told her how pleased we were that Rico liked us. Immediately a bond of friendship blossomed between us, and Rico soon began to run to us and hug and kiss us each time we approached. We met the family and were soon invited to their fiestas where we took pictures, especially of Rico.

Through Dona Juana we met her husband, Julio, a shy, short man who sells fruit and vegetables from door to door in Cuernavaca. He, in turn, introduced us to his father, an ancient Native American who treasures his rural culture, which he fears he is losing by living in the city, and so he makes every attempt to pass on to his grandchildren the stories, songs, dances, and language of his ancestors.

After a few months, Dona Juana began to give Rico a small plastic bag of fruit to present to us before we caught the bus home in the evenings. How touched we were by this generosity and show of friendship. In return, Patty made oatmeal cookies for Petra and Chonita and for Rico's family. They made a hit with everyone and her cookies became famous treats.

From the first day we arrived at La Nopalera for Mass, we had made a conscious effort not to push our way into the lives of the people, as much as we yearned to be accepted. We often commented that we thought it would take years, if ever, for the people to accept our presence completely. Though it made us sad, and at times very anxious, we accepted the fact that we might never be welcome and that the people might resent our efforts to become part of their community.

After six months of visiting, we had, we felt sure, begun to be accepted. First it was by the children who were moved by curiosity but were able nonetheless to reach out to us. They introduced us to their mothers and grandmothers who shyly welcomed us into their homes and in time introduced us to their husbands.

We were far from our goal of understanding and embracing the spirit of the poor but we were making progress. The most discouraging and exhausting days were behind us. We were no longer strangers, and for the time being that was enough. We often reflected on our first Sundays there and how moving the services were for us.

The People's Determination

In those first few months, we were simultaneously struggling with our adjustment to life in the Third World and trying to understand the people we met in La Nopalera. We talked together endlessly about each encounter and gradually came to a few conclusions, obvious to us now, but then they were significant revelations.

The people in La Nopalera worked hard and still they were poor. The old myths of Mexicans sleeping in the sun under the shade of huge sombreros were clearly not true. Men left their homes at 5:00 in the morning and did not return until late in the evening. They worked six days a week, had no protection against accident or illness, and were paid barely enough to live. Many women, like the ancient Chonita, had small stores they opened early in the morning and kept open until after 9:00 in the evening. Most had built their homes themselves, working on Sundays or when they were laid off. Many had to carry water to their homes in addition to washing clothes by hand; they had to fight endlessly against the dust that covered everything within a few hours. In spite of all this, the people were clean. We had to marvel that mothers kept their children so clean in such circumstances. There was little or no public drunkenness, although people hinted at hidden cases here and there in the community. They also said that drugs were a problem among some of the youth but if they were, we witnessed no public display of violence or withdrawal. Later we would stumble upon deadly violence, but here, in this place, violence did not seem to be a problem.

The Cause of Poverty

Gradually we came to understand that the myths about poverty so many believe were simply not true here. These were poor people but not lazy or careless or addicted. Why, then, were they so poor? We asked that question of scholars and of the people themselves.

Scholars talked about the international debt, the decline in prices of raw materials, international banking policies, and arcane fiscal policies. In his opening address to the Latin American bishops gathered in Puebla, Mexico, in 1978, Pope John Paul II said:

Analyzing this situation more deeply, we discover that this poverty is not a passing phase. Instead it is the product of economic, social, and political situations and structures, though there are other causes for this state of misery. In many instances this state of poverty within our countries finds its origin and support in mechanisms which, because they are impregnated with materialism rather than any authentic humanism, create a situation on the international level where the rich get richer at the expense of the poor who get even poorer.[2]

The people had a simpler explanation. "It is the rich," they said, "who have taken all our country's wealth and left nothing for us. Our enemy is not the United States or Japan or even our own government. Our enemy is the rich. They control these governments, of course, and the governments do what the rich want. Our own is no different from the others. The powerful men in Mexico City do not care about us. All they want is money for themselves and their families. They live in big houses, have big swimming pools, drive big cars, and make big promises, but here we are worse off than our fathers and mothers ever were."

These simple people have never heard of economics or economic theory but they understand that the world is divided into two classes, the rich and the rest of humanity. You could call their analysis Marxist or Communist perhaps, but it also seemed to us to echo the words of Mary's "Magnificat."

He has shown the power of his arm,
he has routed the proud of heart.
He has pulled down the princes from their thrones
and exalted the lowly.
The hungry he has filled with good things,
the rich sent empty away. (Luke 1:50–53)

Whether you dress the reality in economic or religious terms, the facts remain the same. This world is sharply divided into the rich and the poor. Statisticians tell us that 4 out of 5 people in the world are poor and in Mexico the number is 7 in 10. Marx was right, in part at least. There are two classes and in spite of incredible scientific and technological progress since the beginning of the Industrial Revolution, the poor are getting poorer and they know this is true. Here we were discovering the root of revolution: the growing discontent with things the way they are. There was much for us to ponder.

The idea of assigning guilt to a whole class of people, however, went against our grain. Granted that there were two classes in the world, one rich and the other poor, how could millions of people in rich nations be guilty? They were and are unaware of the problems of the world's poor. We ourselves were only beginning to awaken to the immensity of the awful reality. Was it fair to blame the rich for the problems of the poor?

We were struggling with this contradiction when we stumbled upon Saint Peter's second sermon recorded in the Acts of the Apostles. In this story Peter and John have just healed a man who was crippled from birth. The cure causes great excitement in the Temple where hundreds of loyal Jews have come for regular prayer. This is what Peter says to them:

> You are Israelites, and it is the God of Abraham, Isaac, and Jacob, the God of our ancestors, who has glorified his servant, Jesus, the same Jesus you handed over and then disowned in the presence of Pilate after Pilate had decided to release him. It was you who accused the Holy One, the Just One, you who demanded the reprieve of a murderer while you killed the prince of life....Now I know, brothers, that neither you nor your leaders had any idea what you were really doing; this was the way God carried out what he said through his prophets that his Christ would suffer. Now you must repent and turn to God so that your sins may be wiped out...(Acts 3:13–20).

Peter said four things:

1. The entire Jewish people [living at that time] were responsible for the death of Jesus,

2. even though they and their leaders acted in ignorance;
3. and so they must repent and turn to God,
4. so that their sins might be wiped out.

There it is, the condemnation of a whole class of people (the Jewish people) even though they were unaware of what they were doing. The only cure Peter could offer them was repentance and then, and it seems only then, would their sins be wiped out. They were told to repent for what they had done in ignorance, which sounds strange to our modern, individualistic ears. We think of sin as something individuals do, not something for which whole groups are responsible. Yet, here it is, in one of our most ancient Christian texts, a treasured memory of that first generation of believers.

Saint Peter's argument is unsettling for most moderns. At first blush it seems unfair to lump together a whole people and attribute guilt to them. Our difficulty with this kind of thought arises from the almost exclusive focus of our moral theology in recent centuries on the individual, thus ignoring the idea of social sin. While we continue to acknowledge the importance of group attitudes, values, and actions, we call this examination sociology, not theology or ethics. Bible writers made no such distinction. For them the actions, values, and attitudes of both groups and individuals were a matter of moral concern. One of the most interesting and controversial teachings of today's liberation theology is its return to this biblical pattern of thought. In trying to understand the inner workings of groups and the reasons why they behave as they do, these theologians have often had to use ideas and insights taken from non-Christian sources because traditional Christian theology has in the recent past ignored this side of human activity.[3]

The notion that the world's rich had once more condemned Jesus in the poor, even though they did not realize what they were doing, seemed to reflect the thought of Peter. Therefore, we too must repent if our sin is to be forgiven. Repentance in the case of

Peter and in our own situation today means disassociating ourselves from the class that has done wrong and becoming a part of
those who are oppressed. No matter how fearful traditional theologians may be of this emerging class consciousness and struggle,
it exists among the poor, and ironically the justification for it is
clear in the Christian Scriptures. Pope John Paul II seems to echo
these thoughts in his latest encyclical, *Centesimus Annus:*

> Too many people live not in the prosperity of the Western
> world, but in the poverty of the developing countries amid
> conditions which are still a yoke, little better than slavery it-
> self. The church has felt and continues to feel obliged to de-
> nounce this fact with absolute clarity and frankness, know-
> ing that its call will not always win favor with everyone.[4]

Generosity

Let us shout this: the people in La Nopalera were generous. Because there was no welfare of any kind, they supported their
neighbors who were unable to work. They took in children whose
parents had died or abandoned them. They never hesitated to
share what little they had with us who did not need the gifts they
offered. Unlike the people we had grown up with and lived our
adult lives among, these people saw generosity, not financial success, as their most important virtue. The key role of generosity in
the development of personality among the poor shocked us at
first. It was so different from anything we had ever seen before.

One day we met a beautiful women in her fifties bent over the
side of the road picking up bits of corn that had dropped from a
passing truck. She told us that she was taking them for her chickens. One thing led to another in our relationship and in a few
months she had learned to read, joined one of our favorite base
communities, and married a local widower. Together they built a
tar-paper shack in which to begin their married life. We gave
them an inexpensive gift for their new home. The next week, Rosa
Carmina and her new husband appeared at the base community

meeting with not one but two shawls for Patty, so moved had she been by our kindness and so determined to share generously with us.

It seemed that the less people had, the more generous they became. Nowhere is this inclination to generosity more obvious than in the way they treat children. Simply put, they love children and do not hesitate to make big sacrifices for them. Old men and women whose own children are raised and whose resources are tightly limited take long-lost cousins into their homes. Parents with five or six children of their own do not hesitate to "adopt" another parentless child or two. Most men are just as tender with children as women are. The buses are full of men carrying their little ones. Children are not spanked in public and as far as we can see rarely in private either. Parents seem unconcerned about their children's success in school and demanded only that they respect and love other children and the adults around them. This, too, gave us great pause for thought.

The word "generosity" comes from the Latin word meaning tribe or perhaps community. Thus, the generous person is one who cares about the community and especially about its future. The great American psychologist Erik Erikson used a similar word, "generativity," to describe the response of the mature to the challenges of life. In both these words, we see a longing for men and women who care about the community, especially about its youngest and most vulnerable members.

This love of children, so much a part of the people of La Nopalera, flew in the face of the assumptions of many of our friends from North America who visited us. Once they had viewed the poverty of the people, they immediately asked about birth control and assumed that the reason for the large families was the teaching of the Roman Catholic church. The American assumption was that there would be less poverty if there were more birth control, and that the Catholic church stood in the way of any progress in this regard.

This kind of reasoning made sense, or at least it seemed to. If there were fewer children, each child should have more. And, it was true that official church policy condemned all but the most difficult forms of birth control. We ourselves wondered about birth control and its importance in La Nopalera although we were committed to watch and learn from the poor, not to give them our answers to their problems.

One Sunday at a meeting of married couples we discovered that the topic was birth control. A medical professional patiently explained all the ways birth control could be achieved: the pill, the diaphragm, the condom, the IUD. People listened attentively and agreed that birth control was a good thing since it was hard to raise many children here in the city, much harder than it had been in the campo. Someone tentatively expressed the thought that church leaders opposed birth control. Others questioned whether these rich, unmarried men could understand their problems. No one really seemed to worry about church leaders. To them, these men were not a problem.

There were other problems, however, ones that we had not thought about before. One old man put these into perspective when he said, "We do have fewer children now than we used to have, but we are poorer now than we used to be. When you have fewer children, the bosses just lower your salary. You end up without much of a family and without any money either. The only ones who get richer are the bosses."

The group nodded in agreement. This had been their experience, too. We later learned that in Mexico the rate of reproduction had been reduced by half in 25 years and yet the per capita income had plummeted. Perhaps birth control might be a step toward reducing poverty, but the poor believed that their poverty was caused much more by the greed of a few rich than by the poor's desire for unlimited reproduction. They had been promised a better life if they had fewer children. Now their families were both smaller and poorer. They felt victimized not by their church, which did not seem to understand their problems, but by the rich, who exploited them.[5]

Women agreed that finances were no better with smaller families, but they reminded all of us that women's health had improved as a result of having fewer children. They also remarked that they were better able to care for their children than their mothers had been when they often had ten or more children. We listened intently and were happy that we had not offered our solutions to their problems of poverty. We did wonder, however, how we North Americans had been convinced of such a simplistic answer to the world's poverty problem. We wondered, too, who had decided that we should never know the poor people's side of the story. Was it perhaps true that the real reason for our American interest in the worldwide use of birth control was an effort to preserve the goods and services we need for our own rich lifestyle and to protect our national security? This is the argument of Peter J. Donaldson, a U.S. population control expert, in his book *Nature Against Us: The United States and the World Population Crisis, 1965-1980.*[6] It sounds very much like the reasons alleged by many for our intervention into the Kuwait-Iraq conflict. We had to wonder if the poor understood this problem better than we did. It seemed to be one more reason for their desire for a revolutionary change in the way the world works (or doesn't).

Our poor friends were concerned with survival problems, the kind most middle-class North Americans rarely, if ever, encounter. Their water supply was undependable and polluted. Obtaining sufficient food was a daily challenge, so much so that 84% of the people in Cuernavaca and the surrounding state never drink milk, 75% never eat meat, 63% cannot afford eggs, and almost 10% are afflicted with gastro-intestinal disease from which one in five die.[6] The food problem is a result of soaring inflation, low wages, and high unemployment. Add to these problems alcoholism, drug abuse, and an oppressive and corrupt police force and you have some vision of why problems such as some churchmen's attitude toward birth control seem unimportant.

Our Situation

Thus our first months with the poor at La Nopalera came to an end with many questions and few answers. We knew that when the answers arrived, they would be as important for us and our lives as they are for the poor themselves. About this time we began to cut our ties with other projects and devote our full time to our new friends in La Nopalera. We sensed that the revelation we had come to Mexico to find was breaking in upon us as we learned more and more about the spirit of the poor.

—Chapter Four—

Education, Mexican Style

*We join our first small groups, begin to form friend-
ships, and discover the radical discontent that seethes
beneath the calm Mexican exterior.*

In July 1990, when we returned from our first trip back to the
United States, we discovered something new in La Nopalera, a
basic adult education class. We enrolled as students and soon realized that many adults in the community neither read nor wrote
nor had ever been to school.

Until recently, schooling in Mexico was reserved for the rich.
As far back as the time of President Juarez, just after the American
Civil War, the Mexican government began to make impressive
statements about education, but as late as 1975 the average adult
had attended school for fewer than six years. The poor, especially
those in rural areas, were lucky to attend school for one or two
years. Since most of the people in La Nopalera had come from the
campo, few had had more than a year or two of formal education
and many had never attended school at all.[1]

Learning Anew

Our adult education class began with six students, including the two of us. We sat on rickety, rush chairs in an open area outside the sisters' house. For several weeks we did nothing but copy the letters of the alphabet. Bill was at the bottom of the class for, try as he might, he could not form his letters to suit the young Mexican teacher. This endeared him to the other students who frequently tried to help him.

In spite of our academic difficulties, we were—to our surprise—soon helping many people read and write in Spanish, although our own Spanish was barely functional. This task was thrust upon us when after the first month the teacher whom the government had sent rarely came to class. Everyone in the group, from Arnulfo who is 83 years old to Rocio, a 15-year-old school drop-out, thought it very funny that we could read and write Spanish but often did not understand what the words meant. They, on the other hand, had to sound out each syllable laboriously, but understood the meaning of the words quite clearly.

It was a happy combination and we looked forward to our Monday and Friday afternoons at the *escuelita*, our little school, which soon numbered twenty students. The "classroom" was no more than two small white tables with chairs dragged out into the yard from the church. Fortunately, the sisters had planted bougainvilleas when they arrived in 1983 and we found some relief from the intense sun under the shade of the ever-flowering vines. Here more than education was happening. We were making friends and entering more and more deeply into the lives of the Mexican poor. In this strange classroom we sensed that we were drawing closer to the spirit of the poor, the revelation we sought and longed for.

New Friends

The little school brought us into deeper contact with many people we might otherwise never have met. Five students who deeply influenced us during these early days were Arnulfo, Maria de la

Paz, Julia, and a young couple, Jesus and Soltera. Each of them taught us something different about the spirit of the poor.

At 83 Arnulfo works every day and comes to class with his reading and arithmetic books tucked in a plastic bag with his ever-present machete. He looks so youthful in spite of his years and hard work that we wondered if he had not drunk from the fountain of youth. From the first day, we knew we had a good friend in Arnulfo who always greeted us with a big hug, standing on tip-toe in his worn-out, dust-covered sandals because he, like most poor Mexican men, is not much more than five feet tall.

There was an unaffected simplicity about Arnulfo. He never hesitated to speak what was in his heart. You knew immediately what he understood and what he did not. He never pretended. Since he does not hear very well, he had to struggle to understand our names. "Bill" was too difficult for him to remember so Bill tried to explain that his real name is William, or Guillermo in Spanish. "Ah," said Arnulfo, *"Tu nombre es Memo."* Your name is Memo, pronounced may-mo. The name stuck first with the class and then with all the people in La Nopalera, and finally even Patty began not only to call Bill Memo but to think of him as that new person.

Bill was overjoyed with his new name and said he felt like Simon must have when Jesus bestowed on him the name Peter, or like Saul when he became Paul. For both of us, Bill's change of name was a profound and mystical experience, for it reminded us that we were entering a whole new life, the life of the poor in La Nopalera. No longer were we burdened with degrees, books to be written, and deadlines to be met. Bill said he was beyond all that, now that he was simply Memo.

Patty became Paty, spelled almost the same but with a very different sound in Spanish, like pah-ti. With our new names, we were beginning to feel a little bit Mexican. First the children, and then the adults, began to call out as we approached, "Here come Paty and Memo." To hear it still sends shivers of joy through our bodies. We know that this gift came to us from our friend, Arnulfo, the old man who always spoke what he believed was true.

Then there was Maria de La Paz, a single grandmother, who came with her daughter Griselda, a primary school drop-out, and her granddaughter, Anna, who was twelve, bright, and already in junior high school. Always smiling and laughing at the slightest provocation, Maria de la Paz immediately took an interest in us and all the other students, or *companeros* as Arnulfo called us. Maria was a natural community-builder and kept us plugging along by her example. Learning to read and write came hard to her, but every Monday and Friday she opened her reading or arithmetic book and sounded out the words, ever so slowly, syllable by syllable, as Patty watched with approval. When she reached the end of each sentence, she would look up, take a deep breath and smile as if to say, "We made it, didn't we?" Then she would doggedly tackle the next sentence.

One day in October a Native American-looking couple with a baby appeared at our literacy class. Their names were Jesus and Soltera; their baby, also Jesus, was ten months old. They were so shy they would not sit at the two small tables we borrowed from the sisters. Instead, they sat apart on a low wall nearby with the little one who could not yet walk clinging to his father's legs or nursing at his mother's breast. Bill took an immediate interest in the couple and in his halting Spanish introduced himself and asked their names and where they lived. Before the day was ended there was a bond of friendship. They began to come faithfully, with Bill as their principal teacher since they still would not join the group.

Jesus and Soltera had come from the mountains of Guerrero in search of work and lived in the newest colonia, Primero de Mayo. Jesus worked cultivating roses on a farm nearby while Soltera remained at home with *el bebe*, the baby, as they both called the handsome and healthy-looking Jesus.

As soon as Bill gained their confidence, they told him that they wanted to learn to read and write so they could help little Jesus when he went to school. Jesus had never been to school and Soltera had been for only a year.

Still sitting apart from the group, Jesus and Soltera made rapid progress. Within weeks they were reading and doing elementary arithmetic. Each day Patty greeted them, tried to make friends with shy little Jesus, and gently invited them to join the larger group, but they continued to refuse—until one day in November when the group was talking about the need to develop into a community. People said that we should be a group that helps one another instead of just coming as individual students relating only to the teacher and the material in the books.

Jesus and Soltera were listening from the sidelines, but the next time they came they brought their chairs over to sit with the rest of us. That was a big day for Bill, for them, and for the whole group. Soon Maria de La Paz took them under her ample wing, and Griselda and Anna succeeded in getting Jesus to leave his mother's lap to play with them briefly.

From Arnulfo we had learned the charm of utter simplicity among the poor. From Maria de la Paz we understood how determined these people were to learn more about the world, and from Jesus and Soltera we soon grasped how intelligence could easily be hidden under the culture of poverty and neglect.

A Special Family

The star of the literacy class, however, was Julia who had passed the entire primaria exam. The teacher, who pointed to her success and assured everyone that they, too, could accomplish what Julia had, never remained with us long enough to help us. Looking back, it was the best thing that happened to the group because, deprived of a leader, we had to make do and soon we had formed a tight-knit community of people who struggled together to learn what we could. In the process we became genuinely caring friends.

Julia had the composure and presence of an Indian princess. We were immediately drawn to her and soon met her entire family. And what a family they were! Her husband, Hermilo, was a gifted carpenter almost old enough to be her father; he was 59 and she 42. If Julia looked like a princess then surely Hermilo was the Emperor Cuauhtemoc come to life, with his regal posture and gold-filled teeth. As Christmas of 1990 grew nearer and we had come to know the family, we naturally made the comparison with Mary and Joseph, so holy were these people who had come to La Nopalera 15 years before to escape the grinding poverty in the state of Guerrero.

In their small house we met Mago, 21, and Eddie, 19, the oldest of their children. Both were studying engineering at a technical college. Eddie helped his father on weekends with the carpentry work and Mago helped with the housework. Next came Carlos, 16, a handsome young man who was about to graduate from high school. We came to call him "Charlie." Finally, there was Veronica, 13, one of the stars of the church youth group's socio-dramas. Every morning she had to catch the bus at 6:00 to attend junior high school in Cuernavaca, an hour away.

Also living in the house were Hermilo's niece, Chave, 35, and his nephew, Eugenio, 30, who worked alongside Hermilo as a carpenter. Both were orphaned when their mother died while they were small children. As a bachelor, Hermilo took the responsibility of raising them, and when he and Julia married, the two children came with Hermilo as part of the family. In spite of the crowded living conditions, an aura of peace and tranquility permeated the house.

Chave is a clear-eyed and intelligent young woman. When we met her she had quit her job as a bookkeeper because she earned 58 thousand pesos a week, $19 (U.S.), and the company would not give her a raise. We quickly learned that even a talented person like Chave, who has a college degree in public accounting, gets paid very little because the unemployment rate is so high. Managers know there are people waiting to take any job, even for very low wages. Over the next four months we watched Chave search for work before she finally found another job that paid more but demanded she work nights and weekends for no extra pay.

The entire family participated in the activities of the parish of

La Nopalera: from serving as lectors to base community leaders to financial advisors to fund raisers. How they managed to do all this is a mystery that continually unfolds for us. They cooperated, perhaps better than any family we have ever met. This love of family and togetherness was another characteristic of the spirit of the poor.

More Contacts

As we were invited to other homes for meals and celebrations, we met more and more extraordinary people who had learned to live harmoniously in conditions one might well expect would produce violence. Indeed there is violence all around them. More often than not, the people who die—their families and friends bring them in cheap caskets to the church for the sisters to pray over before carrying them on foot to the nearby pantheon or cemetery— are victims of violence, like the young man who was stoned to death or the mother of six who was killed by an errant bullet.

Some neighborhood teenagers who study English in high school asked us to start an English class on Sunday afternoons before Mass. The sisters agreed it would be a good way to meet more young people, so we began in September with five students but soon had to divide the group because it had grown to over thirty before Christmas.

About that time we joined two Christian base communities that meet once a week and began to attend meetings of the couples in the parish. Our time in La Nopalera quickly escalated from one day a week, Sunday, to six. Soon it was clear to us and to the people of La Nopalera that we were there to stay and wanted no more than to be friends and neighbors.

Affirmation

We wondered whether we were going about our task of becoming a part of the community in the right way. Since we had no one to guide us, we could do no more than follow the best instincts of our hearts. Several months later, two remarkable things happened.

The first occurred at a lecture Sisters Fidelina and Mari Duran from La Nopalera gave to a group of North Americans. It was a history of the church as it had evolved over the centuries, from the viewpoint of the poor. The sisters traced church history from the primitive (early) church, to Christendom, to Neo-Christendom, to the people of God of Vatican II, to the emerging church of the poor, the reality of today's Mexico.

At the end of their presentation, we all saw the resemblance between the early church's focus and characteristics and the emerging church of the poor that we were experiencing in La Nopalera. One of the North Americans hesitantly raised a question. "What about those of us who are not poor? Can we be part of this church of the poor?"

"Good question," responded Sister Mari through the translator. "Even we sisters who live very simply among the poor have not experienced what the poor have in exactly the same way. What we say is that we accompany the poor and try to become as much like them as we can."

And then came the words that set us on the edge of our chairs; it was so unexpected, the first inkling we had had of how the sisters saw our role at La Nopalera.

"Though it is difficult, it is possible to become a part of this church of the poor. We've been amazed," continued Sister Mari, "at what has happened with the Colemans. Many people, both Mexicans and North Americans, visit our mission at La Nopalera. Our people are always polite but do not pay much attention. By contrast, I wish you could see them when Memo and Paty come down the street. The children run up to bring flowers, the old women hug them, and crowds gather to talk with them. All of us sisters have been very impressed with the way our people have accepted the Colemans."

We blushed as we tried to absorb what was being said through the translator. Then, with huge smiles on their beautiful faces, both sisters turned to us in approval.

There it was, our first real feedback. We were going to find the spirit of the poor. Our search was bearing fruit. Tears welled in our eyes as we grasped each other's hands. Our happiness was great indeed.

More Affirmation

The second big moment came for us a few months later when Sister Fidelina mentioned casually that the sisters had decided to write about us in an article they were sending to the United States for distribution at Christmas by the brothers of Weston Priory. We wondered what the sisters could have written about us. We couldn't help much since our Spanish was terrible and many days we weren't quite sure what we were doing. The talents we used as writers and catechists seemed useless in this setting.

"Well," we agreed, "as soon as we receive a copy we'll know." It took months before we were able to read what the sisters thought of our work but the months were worth waiting when we read:

> The integration of the Colemans into the community of La Nopalera has been simple and spontaneous, and the people accept them as part of their community, and they themselves feel so at home among the people. It has been a great testimony both to the people and to ourselves how they have come close to the poor and shared their love with them, especially with the children. They have adapted well to the environment, traveling in the small "combi" buses that the people use and making more and more friends each time....

We had spent a year walking the dusty streets of La Nopalera, visiting homes, attending classes, joining Christian base communities, attending church services, playing with the children and listening, listening, listening. But had we found the spirit of the poor? The poor had found us and accepted us. We had begun to make friends and had some insights into the way they looked at life, but we were only beginning to learn and we knew it.

A Bed-Rock Belief

Now we began to understand a basic belief of the poor. It came up again and again in their everyday conversations, in their base community meetings, and even in their music. It was an assumption we had heard before but always in academic circles when professors and students debated the merits of Karl Marx's theories. Juan was the most insightful of the people we met. He read widely and welcomed opportunities to talk about economic theory, but what he expressed in forceful political terms others discussed in less formal or even religious language. They believed that society was divided into two distinct classes, the rich and the poor. The rich exploited and oppressed the poor. Whether it was rich nations or rich individuals made little difference. Oppression was oppression and those who were poor, like the people at La Nopalera, lived under its yoke.

Often discussions were couched in the imagery of the Exodus story in the Bible. The people identified with the freed slaves in the desert and saw the rich, both those in Mexico and in the First World, as the Egyptians. The U.S. president and their own political leaders were the pharaohs, but the guilt of this oppression was spread among all the rich. It was a class problem that would be cured only when the rich class was deprived of its ability to oppress. People talked openly of the need for a revolutionary change.

They also talked about creation as God's gift to all people. No one, they maintained, had a right to be rich while others were poor. Perhaps because they came from a culture based on communal ownership, they believed that capitalism was evil, an evil so violent that it cried to heaven for vengeance. These people were not supporters of the former Russian style of revolution, but neither did they accept the way of life we had been brought up to hold sacred. They no more believed in an unrestricted right of individual ownership than they did in the divine right of kings. We met one young couple, deeply religious and well educated, who had named their first child Marxie. The second was named for

Saint Anthony, another champion of the poor. To them, religion, politics, and economics are one because God is just and loves the poor.

Creation, the Exodus, and the insistent teaching of Jesus about justice and poverty were the linchpins of their faith. Mary, too, was a prophet, especially in the words of the "Magnificat" in which she echoes the promise that God would feed the hungry and send the rich away empty. To these poor people, the Bible was and is a revolutionary document that sustains them in the midst of overwhelming oppression.

Their attitudes are not new ones, nor is their appeal to the ideals of Jesus for relief a new idea. In 1511, ten years before the conquest of Mexico, Antonio Montesinos, a Dominican friar, preached to the rich and powerful on the island of Hispaniola (now Santo Domingo and Haiti):

> I am the voice of Christ crying out in the wilderness of this island and therefore it behooves you to listen to me not with indifference, but with all your heart....This voice declares that you are in mortal sin, and live and die therein by reason of the cruelty and tyranny you practice on these innocent people. Tell me, by what right or justice do you hold these Indians in such cruel and horrible slavery?....Why do you so greatly fatigue them, not giving them enough to eat or caring for them when they fall ill from excessive labors, so that they die or rather are slain by you, so that you may extract and acquire gold every day? ...Are they not human beings? Do they not have rational souls? Are you not bound to love them as you love yourselves?[2]

Population statistics in Mexico highlight how severe the impact of Spanish domination was on the indigenous population. When Hernan Cortez arrived at Veracruz in 1519 there were about 24 million inhabitants in what is now Mexico and Guatemala. By the end of that century, there were fewer than a million. It took until the second quarter of this century for the population to regain the status it had had over 400 years earlier.

Although the circumstances of people's lives have changed over the past 500 years, the same oppression continues and the same arguments against it are still raised. What Fray Montesinos said less than twenty years after Columbus first visited this hemisphere might well be said in any wealthy parish today.

While the poor continue to demand change, they are patient in waiting for it to occur, as they are patient in almost every aspect of their lives. Many mistake this patience for passivity but our experience has taught us that the people of La Nopalera are anything but passive. They work in their political parties, protest each attempt of the bureaucracy to oppress them, and take a lively interest in national and world politics. Some have even gone to Nicaragua or Cuba to help with harvests or to attend conferences of poor people. Many others made sacrifices to support these trips.

There was something more in their attitudes, something beyond dedication and patience, that marked them as very special. They believed in their cause—the coming of the kingdom of God, the need for social change—but this belief never obscured their concern for people. Those who spoke most clearly about the need for a new world order were the very men and women who smiled at children, laughed at their own foibles, and hugged those around them. In their concern for causes, they never lost sight of people.

"Justice Engineers"

About this time, we met a dedicated North American young family who had come to Mexico because they believed in social justice. The parents labored from dawn to dusk, spoke Spanish well, and never hesitated to speak out against the injustices they saw around them. In so many ways, they were an admirable addition to the North American community in Cuernavaca. We introduced them to our poor friends in La Nopalera and were surprised at their obvious unwillingness to accept them into the community.

No matter how often they came among us, and no matter how eloquently they spoke about justice and the coming reign of God, the poor did not seem to trust them or to want them around.

We were perplexed until we spoke about this couple with one of our poor friends. She understood our question even before it was out of our mouths. "Your friends," she began, "are full of anger against injustice, and that is good, but they do not love us just yet. They love their teachings and their ideas, I think, but they do not play with our children, or want to visit our old people, or try to help our broken ones. They know how to be angry but they have not yet learned to cry. We will wait until they learn to love all the little people and then we will be friends."

She was right, of course. Our friends were ideologues, but good ones. They were dedicated to justice but somehow they had little personal warmth, a failing common among even the most committed North Americans. Patty described them as "justice engineers." They entered the field of human relations with the same kind of impersonal solutions that an engineer would use in planning a sewer project.

By contrast, our base community friends put great stock in first building warm personal relationships and then talking about ideas. Greetings were most important. You took the hand of the person you were greeting and held it tight, looked deep into their eyes, and then spoke a greeting as you hugged and kissed them. This took time but it set the tone and reinforced the belief that people are infinitely more important than any ideas or plans. In the meeting you always listened with great interest and respect to anyone who spoke, even if you disagreed. You waited for a natural pause in the conversation before suggesting your own ideas and always phrased them in a way that would not offend those with whom you disagreed.

A Patient Determination

The poor we met each day were determined to bring about social change and believed that the two-tier system in which they lived was unjust. They were also patient waiting for change and always put personal relationships before social planning. These attitudes had profound consequences in their everyday lives.

This belief in two classes, the rich and the poor, infiltrates much of what people believe. Since the rich are unjust and oppressive, few feel that being poor is a personal failure. It is no disgrace to own little. In fact, to own very much is reason to be suspect of dishonesty or betrayal of the community. Being poor is almost a sign of dignity and rectitude.

Success, too, is something different from what it is in North America. Owning or consuming much is not a sign of a successful person. The successful person, the man or woman held in high esteem, respected and offered as a model for the young, is the popular leader, the person who gives much to the community, who is most forceful in working for a change that benefits all. Such leaders rarely own much and are often the object of petty persecution by the powerful, but it is they who command the highest respect in the community.

Oscar Romero, the assasinated archbishop of San Salvador, is a real folk hero. People speak of him as a saint, their saint, a protector of the poor against the rich. They pray easily to the martyrs, not men and women of ancient Rome, but people of our own time who died in the struggle for justice in Central and South America. Most people personally knew a man or a woman who died under mysterious circumstances while proclaiming justice for the poor. Martyrs are very real to the poor in La Nopalera.

One other biblical image that we frequently encountered was the notion of the "kingdom of God." Our training had taught us to identify this with the afterlife, the reward for good and faithful people who had borne the brunt of suffering in this world. To the people of La Nopalera, however, the kingdom of God is something much more contemporary and real. It is the age of justice in which the poor receive a fair share of the world's resources. They see this age dawning wherever people organize to demand their rights in the name of a just and compassionate God.

Some hoped that Cuba or Nicaragua or El Salvador might be the first blush of the kingdom's dawning. Others were more circumspect. All, however, believed that the evil from which they are to be delivered was the oppressive capitalism under which they lived. God, they were sure, wanted that.

It was perhaps these insights that convinced us we were beginning to come close to the spirit of the poor. We now had friends who were poor whom we could speak with openly. We were not always sure we understood everything about poverty, about being poor, but we knew that what we did understand was very different from anything we had heard before.

Capitalism

The spirit of the poor is not a passive dependence on God, but a belief in God's concern for the poor and love for them. Yet, this belief in no way absolves the poor from the struggle for their own liberation. That liberation is, in the minds of most, tied to the radical modification or total suppression of the capitalist system. We had to conclude that to have the spirit of the poor, at least at this time and in this place, one had to oppose the capitalism that has dominated our era of history.

The Roman Catholic bishops of Peru spoke forcefully about capitalism in 1971:

> What has been said before [the lack of participation by workers in capitalism] and the experience lived by our own people lead us to reject capitalism, in its economic expression, as well as in its ideological basis, which favors individualism, profit and the exploitation of humanity by humanity. We should, therefore, aim toward the creation of a qualitatively different society.[3]

From a more radical perspective, we read in *The Road to Damascus* by Third World Christians:

> In our countries, the worship of money, power, privilege

and pleasure has certainly replaced the worship of God. This form of idolatry has been organized into a system in which consumerist materialism has been enthroned as a god. Idolatry makes things, especially money and property, more important than people. It is anti-people. This idol is "anti-people" because it demands absolute submission and blind obedience; it makes its worshippers slaves, prisoners, or robots. Subservience to money dehumanizes people. Profits are pursued at the expense of people. The graven image of the god of money today is the national security state that defends the system and demands absolute obedience. In some countries, it is cruel and merciless; in others, it wears a deceptive mask. Those who disobey are punished brutally; those who obey are rewarded with material benefits and security. Idols rule by fear and intimidation or by trying to buy people, to bribe them and seduce them with money.[4]

Capitalism and the consumerist materialism which is a part of it, however, are so much a part of our lives that it seems almost impossible to imagine life without it. The kind of repressive socialism tried in the Soviet Union for the past seventy years has done little to help the poor. Now, it seems clear, this system has failed massively. Even the Soviet Union is attempting to enter the free market economy. No one can any longer hold up this system as the wave of the future. Our friends in La Nopalera understand this.

The level of political and economic freedom in the United States has been much higher than in the former Soviet Union, and its economic system is capitalistic. On the other hand, Latin America is every bit as repressive as the Soviet Union used to be, and its economic system is capitalistic. Where does that leave us? Our friends in La Nopalera oppose both communism and capitalism as we have seen them in practice; they believe that had Nicaragua been given a fair chance without outside intervention it might have offered an alternative.

It has occurred to us that the accumulation of capital is necessary in our modern world. Actually both communist and capitalist systems have this is common. Where they differ is how each answers these questions: Who should benefit from this capital? Who should control it?

It is patently unfair that a small minority should reap most of the benefits brought by accumulated capital since God made the world for all people. Without jumping to the conclusion that everyone should have exactly the same benefits from the world's riches, we can at least wonder why some people starve while others mindlessly consume. We are told that if this were not so, the rich would no longer work to better the condition of the masses. But who tells us this? We sometimes suspect that it is the rich who employ scholars and the media to convince the rest of us that any change in the present system would bring about great economic tragedy. Perhaps this is not the case at all. Perhaps it is only the rich who would suffer a loss.

Among liberation theologians we detect a profound disillusionment with capitalism as they have experienced it. Many of them remind us that this system is based on greed and, as such, is in open conflict with the gospel. Dorothee Solle, a German theologian heavily influenced by liberation theology in Latin America, says:

> One of the catastrophic consequences of capitalism is what it does to the rich people at the heart of this economic system by reducing humanity to the individual. One can see how American commercialism presents all items as being "quite personal to you," even if millions of them exist. Your initials must be on your T-shirt, on your ball-point pen, on your bag—on your Jesus. He too is quite personal to you. The spirit of commercial culture is also alive in this religion: for fundamentalism, which is massively effective, Jesus is "my personal savior," and really no more can be said than that. The confession of "Jesus Christ—my personal savior" brings

no hope to those whom our system condemns to die of famine. It is a pious statement which is quite indifferent to the poor and completely lacking in hope for all of us.[5]

While the capitalism experienced in Central and South America differs from what most North Americans know, both systems are based on greed. In North America, however, the people have placed some restraints on the system while in Latin America there are few controls. When capitalism operates south of the border, it does so without the restraints it has at home. It allies itself with the most repressive and greedy elements of the Latin American population and creates the impression that all North Americans, and their leaders as well, are intent on repression and exploitation of the poor.

This impression coupled with American intervention in Latin affairs is causing an intense resentment of the U.S. The politics of Nicaragua, El Salvador, Guatemala, Panama, Peru, and other countries are as much directed against the U.S. as they are against injustice in their own nations. It is almost certain that American soldiers will have to continue to sacrifice their lives and those of millions of innocent Latin American campesinos to protect the interests of a relatively few wealthy people.

We North Americans tend to forget our long history of intervention in Central and South America, done most often to protect the interests of American business. Howard Zinn, a U.S. historian, remembers our interventions in the first half of this century:

While demanding an Open Door in China, [the United States] insisted on a Closed Door in Latin America—that is, closed to everyone but the United States. It had engineered a revolution against Colombia and created the "independent" state of Panama in order to build and control the canal. It sent five thousand Marines to Nicaragua in 1926 to counter a revolution, and kept a force there for seven years. It intervened in the Dominican Republic for the fourth time in 1916 and kept troops there for eight years. It intervened for the second time in Haiti in 1915 and kept troops there for nineteen years. Between 1900 and 1933, the United States intervened in Cuba four times, in Nicaragua twice, in Panama six times, in Guatemala once, in Honduras seven times. By 1924 the finances of half the twenty Latin American states were being directed to some extent by the United States.[6]

Unfortunately our record has not improved in the second half of this century. The poor remember this as they gather their own forces together to demand revolutionary change in the structures of capitalism, which oppress and demean them.

Power comes with accumulated capital. In the U.S. constitution, political power, at least, is divided among three groups and they are encouraged to struggle with one another. When each of the three is more or less equal to the other two, the country is healthy. When one assumes too much control, the country goes into a decline. It is good, then, to restrict power by creating several competitive power centers. Perhaps in this simple lesson of history lies the answer to the problem of capitalism in our modern world. We must create governments capable of challenging economic tycoons, school systems that educate a population to withstand the consumerism on which capitalism thrives, and churches that are not afraid to exercise their prophetic function.

Our Situation

Our time with the Mexican poor has called us to try to understand life from their perspective. The questions they raise have become our questions, too, for only in this way can we begin to discover the true spirit of the poor. Our answers to these questions are, however, always tinged with our own First World insights, for we are who we are, an American couple searching to understand that revelation that is already so clear to the Latin American poor.

—Chapter Five—

The Heart of Mexico: The Rutas

We discover the pulse of the poor and experience the stubborn strength born of community, which has the power to demand revolutionary change.

Perhaps nothing so captures the pulse of the Mexican poor as the *ruta* (literally, route), a small 25-seat bus that plies the steep city streets and unpaved backroads of the poorest areas. Rutas are a lifeline for the poor as they make their way to and from work, to shop for groceries and clothes, to receive medical attention, and for the very important ritual of visiting relatives.

The Buses

These are not staid North American buses but brightly decorated, run-down, over-crowded, held-together-with-tape, living organisms in various stages of disintegration. From time to time, a ruta dies along the roadside and we passengers are "sold" to the next one that is going in our direction. All rutas have written on their massive windshields the names of the areas they serve. The list is

changed periodically during the day by the driver, whom Mexicans call the "chofer," who uses great dabs of white shoe polish.
Each ruta route has its own number prominently displayed on the
front and back and is trimmed in its own coded combination of
colors. This is important for those who cannot read.

All the rutas have certain indispensables. Above the massive
windshield is a huge hand-crocheted, fringed, mini-curtain with a
word like Amor woven into it. Besides this there are decals of Our
Lady of Guadalupe and Jesus Crucified, and clustered around
these are more secular decals with slogans or pictures of Disney
characters and pretty women. As you sit, if you are lucky enough
to find a seat, you get a warm, homey feeling as you stare at the
front of the ruta to keep your eyes from noticing the oncoming
traffic and the driver's skillful, dare-devil weaving in and out between buses and cars, a skill that "chofers" are proud of.

Life on the Buses

The drivers are as colorful as the decorations and vary in age
from 18 to 60, all men, most of whom work 12-15 hours a day
driving for rich *duenos*, or owners. Most are friendly and helpful.
One even babysits his 2-year-old boy who stands by his left side,
waving out the window. Once in a while, however, we ride with
what the people call a *diablo*, a devil who drives at double the normal speed.

Above the driver's seat, within easy reach, most have their tape
deck which has ominous looking wires that dangle down and dis-
appear under the control panel. One day we sat directly behind the
driver and saw where the wires went. They joined a tangle of other
wires that were smoking gently. We decided never to look again.

The passengers, too, are fascinating mostly because of their stoic,
calm, expressionless faces and gentle manner. The smallest children, who haven't yet learned the passivity of the adults, smile and
move around on the seats next to the impassive people who ride
with them. With people constantly getting on and off, we shift
seats and crowd together to allow more people to enter. On buses

built to seat 25, it is not unusual to see more than 50 men, women, and children—along with their bags, live chickens, open boxes of rotting vegetables, maize, tortillas and plants—jammed together down the center aisle and hanging out the front and rear doors. No pushing or shoving, just gentle accommodation to the situation.

In spite of the oppressive heat, we have only once smelled body odor and this was an old man who got on with all his belongings strapped to his back. Obviously he was homeless, and bathing, the beloved Mexican pastime, was not possible. All the rest, no matter how shabbily dressed, have made the effort to keep themselves and their children clean and free of body odors.

The music is incessant and loud. Sometimes the songs have English lyrics and we hum along, glad to hear familiar words. Usually, it's rock and roll. When the music stops, we've learned to anticipate live entertainment, for there are bands of actors and musicians who manage to survive on the small donations they receive from passengers. Since all the people on the rutas are themselves poor, this is a true manifestation of their compassion and generosity.

Small children, some as young as 5 years old, jump on if the driver agrees and weave their tiny bodies through the crowds as they sing in strained, raspy voices and accompany themselves by scratching ribbed Clorox bottles with combs. Most of us would pay to have these little fellows stop singing, so discordant is their "music." But our hearts break at the sight of their ragged clothes and the knowledge that perhaps their entire family depends on their begging from morning to night. No school for these young ones—probably no bright future.

Teenage boys and older men come on board to play and sing with guitars and accordions while clowns join us from time to time for a few antics. Some men who sell fruit drinks in plastic bags held closed by rubber bands with straws protruding from their necks join us just long enough to sell their drinks, hop off, and jump on another ruta going the other way to return to their fruit-drink stand.

Blind men are often helped onto the ruta by other passengers and sing in sweet, mellow voices accompanying themselves on homemade guitars. They then feel their way down the aisles, stumbling over the endless bags and boxes, holding out a hat for donations. Other times, men come on the bus and distribute candy to everyone with a note explaining they are deaf and mute and ask for a donation of 30 cents for the candy; those who don't want the candy can give it back. Imagine such a life!

From time to time, the ruta pulls in to a Pemex, Mexico's state-owned petroleum stations, for a fill-up. While the driver is pumping the gas, groups of women parade through the ruta, selling popsicles, gelatins, puddings, candies, and fried pork skin. Men come on with more fruit drinks and whatever they think will sell.

Since we are almost always the only *gringos* on the bus, we often catch people staring at us. We wonder what they are thinking behind those expressionless faces. If we smile and start talking with someone, however, the person will become instantly animated and begin to ask many questions. Others will invariably join in the conversation. Among themselves, they respect everyone's right to privacy unless that person is a friend or neighbor. From many generations of servitude, the poor have learned it is better not to presume intimacy with, as they sometimes say now that we have become friends, people of "better blood," meaning the rich.

The poor Mexican families who ride the rutas are very proud of their children, and even before we could carry on much conversation in Spanish we made friends by admiring the children, especially the babies. This is easy to do because the children are so beautiful, well-behaved, and inquisitive. One evening, Bill was smiling, cooing, and making faces with a baby girl about nine months old. The baby responded to his every gesture and began to jump up and down in her father's arms as she reached across the aisle to try to touch Bill. The parents obviously enjoyed the dynamic and soon the father stood up and placed the baby in Bill's lap. He was surprised and delighted!

"Isn't it something," Patty said, "that these people trust you enough to give you their baby to hold?"

"Yes," Bill said as he laughed and cooed at the baby, "but are they going to take it back when they get off the bus?"

Another night, when the bus back to Cuernavaca was particularly crowded, a woman got on with several children and packages. We were sitting on the front seat so we offered to hold her big bag of bread and gestured to hold the little boy who appeared to be about one and a half years old. Again, to Bill's surprise, the woman handed him the little boy who stood rigidly in his lap, staring most seriously at him and then back at his mother. Slowly, as if in slow motion, the little tyke's eyes began to droop. Still he wouldn't relax enough to sit down. He leaned forward, still rigid, and slept all the way home nestled against Bill's chest.

The Mexican ruta is a respite from the storm of life. Men and women returning from work doze and somehow manage to judge subconsciously by the curves and "topes," concrete speed barriers, when it is time to get off. Perhaps it's in their genes because even the children returning from school appear to sleep until they draw near their neighborhood. Some of the students catch the bus at 5:30 A.M. and return home as late as 7:30 P.M. No wonder they need to sleep on the ruta.

Illness on the Ruta

The ruta sometimes serves as an ambulance because the people are too poor to afford that service. Some get on the bus on the way to the hospital in Cuernavaca bent over double with pain or with open wounds from beatings they have received. They are accompanied by family members, and people give them their seats. One Sunday evening, as we were returning to Cuernavaca, we found a seat on the long bench at the back and a young woman, carrying several large boxes and dragging along three small children, got on at the next stop. Bill gave the exhausted looking woman his place and her children clung to her lap.

When we asked her what she had in the large boxes, she explained that she had been selling bread all day at the recreation and swimming area in Temixco. We commented that it must be very hard to do that with three small children. She looked at us with intensely sad eyes. "We have to eat and I don't have a husband." Bill, who was standing amid the boxes, gave the children some candy and we all settled down as the ruta inched along in the heavy nighttime traffic.

At first we thought the woman, who was leaning back against the rear windshield, was sleeping, but something in the little children's anxious expressions alerted us that she might be sick. Just then, the woman began to rub her extended left arm with her right hand. When we inquired if she was sick, she said she had had heart trouble for three years and sometimes had pains in her arms and chest.

She laid her head back, and we tried to control our panic for we were beginning to think that this woman might be having a heart attack. Suddenly, she moaned and began to pound the left side of her chest with her fist. Her eyes were glazed as she breathlessly tried to explain that her blood pressure was sometimes high and she relieved the pain by beating her chest. The poor children never said a word. Patty asked if she were going to the doctor. "I'll go tomorrow," she replied, "because by the time I take the children home the emergency room will be closed."

With that, we gave the young woman some money, something we almost never do, and asked her to go directly to the emergency room in a taxi. She thanked us profusely; we wanted to take her and the children in our arms, they looked so fragile and pathetic. Then she said, "I have seen you on the ruta before. Don't you work at the church in La Nopalera?" Patty explained that we did and kissed her gently on the forehead as we left the bus. We've never seen the woman and children again but pray for them often. So many young, desperately poor women trying to eke out a living and raise children alone.

The Elderly

Poor Mexicans are never too old to work and the ruta is the perfect place to see the *viejitos*, the little old ones. On their wrinkled and tranquil faces, their clothes, and their calloused, sandaled feet, one can read the history of suffering of their people. The women in their long salt-and-pepper braids, aprons, and modest dresses are by far the most beautiful women in Mexico, if not all the world. Bent and exhausted from endless years of child-rearing and hard work, their eyes betray the fire still smoldering deep inside and their very wrinkles speak of dogged determination. No wonder artists and muralists have struggled to capture their great beauty.

The old men, bent and scarred from hard work and oppression, are equally handsome. Atop their heads they wear wide-brimmed and often ancient campesino hats; their faces are dark and leathery from working in the sun since childhood to plant and harvest crops. Though the circumstances of life have transplanted them to the periphery of the city, they maintain their farmer's demeanor and love of the land as they haul and drag onto the ruta the fruits and vegetables they will sell in a small store or cart in their neighborhood.

These old men and women are the survivors, the living history of the "Indios," as they call themselves. When we were able to understand more Spanish, we began to talk with these viejitos and hear stories about their own lives and the lives of their ancestors. We have discovered remarkable compassion, faith, wisdom, generosity, hope, and strength among these people who would probably be, in any First World culture, residing in a nursing home or retirement complex.

Always, our conversations with the viejitos end with embraces and a wish to meet again, *Si Dios quiere* (If God wills it). Sometimes our ruta encounters with old people have lead to visiting them in their homes and even to inviting them to come to the Sunday celebration in La Nopalera. We met Rosita on the ruta one day as she struggled to get off the bus with three heavy crates of rotting tomatoes and cabbage leaves. Bill helped her get her crates to the sidewalk and Patty followed since it was also our stop. Then Bill asked Rosita where she lived and, in typical Mexican fashion, she waved one hand about in the air indicating the general direction. Bill turned and said in English, "This woman can't possibly carry these crates. We'll have to go with her."

With that, we explained in Spanish that we were going to accompany her to her house and rearranged our bags so we could help with the crates. "What," we wondered, "is she going to do with all this rotten food?"

"Where did you get all this food?" Patty asked. Rosita explained that she goes to the central market in Cuernavaca several times a week to get food for her *maranos*, food the vendors throw away. She then drags the boxes to the bus stop, loads them into the aisles of the ruta, rides home, unloads her cargo onto the sidewalk where neighbors guard them as she hauls the boxes one by one the three blocks to her house.

"What is a marano?" Patty ventured.

With that, Rosita laughed, revealing an almost toothless grin. "You don't know what maranos are? I'll show you." She shook her head and braids in disbelief. After walking three blocks in the mid-afternoon heat, Rosita approached an old iron-coil bedspring that served as a gate. She welcomed us to her small house and yard. "Careful," she kept repeating, as she shooed chickens, goats, dogs, and cats away from the narrow entrance. Still dragging the crates, we made our way through the animal dung to a fenced area where Rosita proudly announced, "These are maranos." They were large hogs that almost tore down the flimsy wire fence to get to the rotting tomatoes.

We admired the hogs and started picking our way back to the entrance but Rosita would have none of that. "Sit down," she motioned as she dragged two child-sized cane chairs from her shack to the yard. We peeked inside and saw mounds of old clothes and shoes piled to the ceiling. Rosita had broken our illusion that all Mexicans are clean and odor-free. She reeked of a variety of animal odors as she sat down on a rock next to a charcoal stove. The kittens and dogs climbed all over her with obvious affection as she answered our questions about her life.

Rosita, who appeared to be around 70, is pure Mixteca from the state of Oaxaca and has survived her husband and 6 children, whom she spoke of with nostalgia and resignation. After asking us where we came from and why we liked La Nopalera, she brought out a small plastic bag and placed in it 4 newly-laid eggs. "This," she announced with delight, "is for your supper."

Since that first visit, we have become good friends with Rosita and her animals, and she now meets us from time to time on the corner where we get on the ruta. There she shares our attention with little Rico whom we described in Chapter Three. We have met many other viejitos, none quite so eccentric as Rosita, but all equally interesting and generous.

Strength and Patience

Riding on the ruta has put us in touch with the heart of Mexico— the poor—who make up 70% of the population. Bill sometimes says in jest that we live on Ruta 11. There's much truth to that; we spend at least two and a half-hours a day on the ruta, viewing close-up the real life of the poor, with their joys, sorrows, struggles, hopes, and cultural history, just as we observe with our friends in La Nopalera. Each day we learn something new about these noble people. We marvel at their strength and resilience in the face of all the obstacles put in their path by oppression and physical poverty; we marvel that they can still laugh, still believe in a better future through their children, still reach out in friendship and generosity even to strangers like ourselves.

Less than twenty years after the Spanish Conquest, a Franciscan friar, Toribio de Motolinia, who worked in the same area we now live in, described the ancestors of today's ruta-riders. How similar are his discoveries and ours.

There is hardly anything to hinder the Indians from reaching heaven, nothing like the obstacles that hinder us Spaniards and submerge us. The Indians live in contentment although they have so little that they have hardly enough to clothe and nourish themselves....They lose no sleep over acquiring and guarding riches nor do they kill themselves trying to obtain ranks and dignities. They are patient, long-suffering and meek as lambs....Great is their patience and endurance in time of sickness. Their mattress is the hard, bare ground. At most they have only a ragged mat to sleep on and for a pillow a piece of wood....They eat and drink without much noise and talking. They spend their days peacefully and amicably. They seek only what is necessary to sustain life.[1]

That stoic strength remains very much a part of today's Mexican poor as we have experienced them. In our two years of riding the ruta, we have never seen an argument or a display of bad temper. We have yet to see a parent strike a child or even one child hit another. Only the youngest children cry, although many appear exhausted. Both men and women routinely give up their seats to those who appear weak or ill. Those with many bags or packages can expect someone seated to offer to hold the parcels during the long ride. Those who know one another chat amiably and occasionally sing aloud and invite all to join in. When performers and musicians get on the ruta, even the poorest contribute something.

This stoic strength, generosity, and good humor go a long way in explaining why the Mexican poor endure such injustice so patiently. This endurance is certainly one of the marks of the spirit of the poor we have come to understand and embrace. Yet, even the poor have limits to their endurance, and from snatches of conversation we have heard on the rutas we sense that the limits of endurance are being reached.

Most of the people on the rutas are rural people who have fled the countryside not because they wanted to but because life had become impossible there. Many have told us harrowing tales of land take-overs by local *caciques* working for huge agribusiness interests. They have explained that all the choice arable land was used to grow fruit for export to the United States while they were left with poor soil that couldn't support a family. We knew that Mexican agriculture was marginal at best since more than 50% of the country is arid and 32% is semi-arid. Much of the land is too steep for cultivation and thus only 15% of the total land mass of Mexico is considered good farming land. A history of ill-advised and often dishonest land reform has plunged peasants into near despair and caused many of them to move from their traditional homes to the edges of the cities searching for work, any work at all.

While it is true that 2.7 million rural poor have received help from government policies of agrarian reform, there are some 3 to 4 million still awaiting the allocation of plots. Some of the allocations are in the form of *ejido* grants, or communal farms, based on the ancient Native American form of land holding. Often these are unable to be further divided and resist modern forms of agriculture. Thus, they must leave the land and migrate. It is primarily they who make up the 70% of Mexicans who are poor.

Community and Communion

The fact that the poor ride rutas and not in automobiles, as we do in the United States, taught us something important about their sense of community. They are used to being together. Rarely have we heard anyone talk of loneliness, for only rarely is anyone alone. Their small houses are inhabited by children, cousins, grandchildren, aunts and uncles. Their neighborhoods are spilling over with people. Even on the ruta they stand and sit shoulder to shoulder. All of life is spent in community. Poverty insures this for all but a very few. Through centuries of sharing space like this, they have learned simple forms of courtesy and consideration that remove the rough edges from such communal life.

The courtesy that makes community possible is a complex reality. It includes a willingness to respect each person's privacy even when physical proximity makes this difficult. On the rutas we noticed that all but the youngest sit or stand with immobile expressions on their faces. Yet, if you initiate a conversation or if a friend gets on the bus, faces become animated. What appears to be reserve is in reality no more than a ritual of offering others privacy if they want it and of preserving a level of silence necessary for reflection in a crowded world.

Helpfulness is another part of this courtesy. Ruta riders never fail to offer weaker people a seat or to hold their packages for them. Older women will offer to help young mothers while many men do not hesitate to help the elderly on or off the bus. Cooperation seems to be taken for granted. This kind of courtesy sets the stage for community.

Community is an inescapable part of life among the Mexican poor. The physical experience of sharing space provokes profound thought patterns in which people think of "us" rather than "me." The old woman who reflects on the shortage of water does so instinctively in terms of her family, the children in the neighborhood, and the whole community. She never expresses her concern about the water shortage in terms of her own needs or her own inconvenience. The young man organizing people to resist exorbitant government taxes speaks of what the increases will mean to the poorest, to the elderly, and to the weak in the community. He would be considered rude and callous if he appealed to what damage they might do to him or to others as individuals.

In religion, too, this sense of community is paramount. Rarely will you hear someone speak of his or her own personal relationship with God or call Jesus his "personal savior." That such a personal relationship with God exists cannot be denied, but the expression of the relationship is always in terms of growing closer and more involved in the life of the community. God is the God of the community, and only because of the needs of the community does God favor individuals with special gifts.

One of those gifts is "communion," not the sacrament that is a sign and symbol of it, but communion itself, an intimacy among the people. Our own mission at this point was, we realized, to enter into this kind of communion with the poor of Mexico, to become as much as we could one of them, flesh of their flesh, bone of their bone. Our mission was more mystical than we had imagined it could be. When we read Gustavo Gutierrez, the father of liberation theology, we now understand what he meant.

Encounter with Christ in the poor person constitutes an authentic spiritual experience. It is the life of the Spirit, the bond of love between Father and Son, between God and human being, and between human being and human being. It is this profound communion that Christians involved in a concrete historical liberation praxis strive to live—in a love for Christ in solidarity with the poor, in faith in our status as children of the Father as we forge a society of sisters and brothers, and in the hope of Christ's salvation in a commitment to the liberation of the oppressed.[2]

To experience the Mexican poor is to experience something of the wonder and beauty of God. Only God could create people strong enough to withstand the injustice and indignity the world heaps upon them every day of their lives. Only God could make it possible for us to hear the whispers of discontent all around us. We constantly asked ourselves why the poor in Mexico were so different from the poor in the ghettoes of the United States. There are, of course, many reasons for this difference. One is the sheer number of poor in Mexico. In the U.S. to be poor is to be a part of a despised minority while in Mexico being poor places you in the majority. Poverty in the U.S. is a personal defeat while here it is no more than an accident of birth. In the U.S. the poor live far from the rich and have little contact with them, but in Mexico, the poor and the rich are constantly in contact with each other, one being servant to the other. All things considered, we came to realize that poverty in Mexico was better than poverty in the U.S.

because here the poor have not been deprived of dignity and hope.

As we step from the ruta each day, we do so with great pride. We understand that God has given us a small share of the people's strength and ears to hear what they are saying. More and more, we are tasting a unique revelation of God; we are more and more prepared for the poor's revolution when it comes.

Chapter Six

The First of May: A New Poverty

We discover a new level of poverty and begin to reflect on the meaning of human liberation and its role in base Christian communities.

Panchita

La Nopalera was eighteen years old. We often wondered what life had been like when the settlement was new. It seemed an idle question we might never answer until early in December 1990, when we met Sister Francesca, a beautiful young woman known as "Panchita." Returning to La Nopalera after an assignment in another part of Mexico, her task was to begin a mission in the newest and poorest of the colonias, Primero de Mayo, founded just three years before. We asked to go with her during the early phases of her work since several of the people in our literacy class lived there and were starting a base Christian community of their own.

Two days later we found ourselves walking down a rock-filled, dirt road crowded with shy, undernourished children. On the side of the road, clustered here and there were 55-gallon oil drums, partly filled with water. Some were covered with sheets of plastic, but children were playing with some and cattle were drinking from others. This was the only drinking water for the 2000 people who lived in Primero de Mayo. It was delivered by truck every third or fourth day—when there were no problems. On this day water had not been delivered in eight days. Although the water is officially free, people pay as much as a dollar for each barrelful, almost one-third of the official daily minimum wage.

The road hugged a hill. On one side cattle grazed, while the other side dropped off precipitously into a deep ravine. Looking down, we saw tar-paper and stick lean-tos and a few cinder-block dwellings clinging to the hillside. So steep was the pitch that we could not see the huts near the bottom of the hill. The only brick structure in sight in the colonia was a half-finished municipal building which stood forlorn among the mass of impoverished huts.

Sister Panchita explained that Primero de Mayo, occupied three years earlier by the poorest of the poor, mostly people from the neighboring state of Guerrero, is part of the city of Cuernavaca. Yet, it has no electricity or sewers. "Muy feo, muy triste. Very ugly, very sad," sister kept repeating. It was ugly and sad indeed.

Water

We saw children and old men and women climbing up the ravine burdened with large buckets of water. The people washed their clothes in the stream and bathed there far below, and then had to haul water for cooking up the impossible slope to their houses. When the water truck had not come and the barrels were empty, the people drank the stream water that had been polluted by animal and human excrement as well as by chemicals from washing clothes.

Patty asked about the people's health, especially the children's. Sister shook her head and told us that most of the people are sick much of the time and that many of the small children die of dysentery.

Bill wondered where the people bought food, since the colonia was a long way from even a small grocery store and there were no cars or trucks.

Sister explained. "They have to carry everything from neighboring colonias. See those women coming toward us with the plastic shopping bags? They and their young children have to climb down the ravine, labor up the other side, and shop in a market in the next colonia. Then they have to retrace their steps with what they have bought."

"Do the people ever get enough to eat?" Bill continued.

"Probably no one who lives here has an adequate diet. How they manage to survive is a mystery to me. Over half the men are unemployed, most adults are illiterate, and they become very discouraged living in this forsaken place," sister observed.

"What a life these women have," Patty commented, "hauling water, washing clothes and bathing their children in the stream, carrying food from distant markets, and then worrying about the family getting sick from living in such unsanitary conditions."

"And," sister added, "it's a violent place, filled with political factions, alcoholism, and even some drugs. Imagine parents trying to raise children in this environment."

We looked up where we were walking and saw electrical lines hanging from make-shift poles. They hung so low that a small child could reach up and touch them. Sister explained that some clever people had "borrowed" electricity from the power lines in nearby La Nopalera.

We had always felt special compassion for children who suffer from poverty and the little ones at Primero de Mayo touched us deeply. They stood along the road in little groups staring at us as we passed with Sister Panchita. When we greeted them with smiles and *Buenas tardes,* most smiled back shyly. With their clothes hanging torn and limp on their skinny bodies, they lacked the animation you see among healthy children.

Friends

As we continued along the road, we heard a voice from down

below calling, *"Hola, hola, Memo y Paty."* We looked down and saw our friend Maria de la Paz from our literacy class waving from one of the tar-paper huts.

We waved back and shouted, "We thought you lived in La Nopalera."

"I do, I do," Maria shouted back, "but Griselda and I come here to be with Anna." We knew Anna was Maria's 12-year-old granddaughter whose parents had abandoned her. "Come down to visit," Maria beckoned. We explained that we were headed for Jesus and Soltera's house and would come back another day.

Soon we left the road and started down a steep path to the small house where Jesus, Soltera, and little Jesus lived. Along the way, sister looked terrified that one or both of us might trip and tumble to the stream far below. Bill told sister not to worry, that he was *Memo Chivo,* Billy the goat.

Our friends were startled to see us at their door and ushered us into their two-room house. Jesus beamed as he embraced Bill; we could feel how honored he was that we had come with sister to visit them. Soltera invited us to sit down on the double bed in the corner, the only place to sit in the dirt-floored but clean and organized room.

Little Jesus, timid and just learning to walk, stood by his father's side staring at us. Then he pointed toward the corner where we noticed in the dim light from the lone window a shrine with a large framed picture of Our Lady of Guadalupe surrounded by tin cans of flowers, some fresh and some wilted. We must have looked surprised, because Sister Panchita hastened to explain that during the first two weeks of December, leading up to the feast day on the 12th, the picture of Our Lady of Guadalupe along with flowers is carried in solemn procession from house to house throughout the colonias. The day before, the picture of Our Lady had arrived at Jesus and Soltera's house for the night. We could see how honored they were to receive it.

Soltera hurried off to the tiny kitchen with her aunt, Leobalda, who lives on the other side of the ravine, to prepare *atoli,* a popular drink made of corn and water. Meanwhile Jesus showed us the construction he was doing to enlarge the house.

Before returning to La Nopalera, we descended to the bottom of the ravine with sister and Soltera's aunt, stepping between piles of human excrement as we reached the bottom. There we talked with women bathing their children and washing their clothes, while cows, goats, dogs, and chickens drank from the dribble of water that overflowed a small dam.

As dark descended, we scurried back up the ravine, getting a full view of the small huts clinging to the hillside. Leobalda insisted that we return soon to visit her house which was perched alone on top of the opposite side of the ravine.

The Church and the Poor
We left sister and returned to Cuernavaca, riding a roller coaster of emotions after our introduction to Primero de Mayo. As we reflected on our visit, we suspected that this place would become a very important part of our journey. It did more than tell us what La Nopalera had been a decade and a half earlier; it dramatized for us the depths of poverty in which Third World people live today.

Since that first day, we have returned many times to Primero de Mayo. We have joined a base community there, visited many families, and even helped investigate ways of obtaining clean water for the community. What struck us most was the universal belief that life with all its problems is much better in Primero de Mayo than it had been in the campo from which they came.

These poor people also struck us with their endurance. Without complaint, they accepted physical deprivation, the constant illness, the frequent deaths of their children, the violence of some of the young men, and the prevailing sense that life was not likely to get much better—ever. A psychologist might have said that the people of Primero de Mayo were depressed. The sisters who worked with them said that they had not yet discovered what it means to be children of God. Since the days of the Conquest, 500 years earlier, the church had never done more than give them a few sacraments and counsel them to accept their lot in life. If this was the religion Marx once called the opiate of the people, we had to agree with him.

Looking at the European situation during the last century as society struggled to accumulate the capital necessary to launch the industrial revolution in earnest, Marx took a dim view of the teaching of traditional Christianity. Of the church in those times, he wrote:

> The social principles of Christianity preach the need of a dominating class and an oppressed class. And to the latter class they offer only the benevolence of the ruling class. The social principles of Christianity point to heaven as the compensation for all crimes that are committed on earth. The social principles of Christianity explain all the viciousness of oppressors as just punishments for original sin or other sins, or as trials the Lord, in his infinite wisdom, inflicts on those the Lord has redeemed. The social principles of Christianity preach cowardice, self-hatred, servility, submission, humility—in a word, all the characteristics of a scoundrel.[1]

Closer to our own day, in 1988 a group of Christian theologians reflecting on the religious situation in Central America wrote something similar but, for the churches at least, perhaps more damning:

> In the process of maturing in their historical consciousness with the help of their faith, Central America's poor have come to find out that the God of Western Society was not the God of Jesus, but rather an idol of the Empire. They realized that God does not want the present system (even if it is blessed by the institutional churches), but a new order that implies the destruction of the old.
>
> Based on their faith they rose up, and are still rising up

against the old society called "Christian"; they rose up against the God that was supposedly Christian. But they did not do it in the name of atheism or against religion. Rather they appealed explicitly to that God whom Jesus revealed to us, the God whom Jesus rediscovered as unmistakably the God of the poor and of life.[2]

We sensed that we are not alone in our distrust of traditional Christian churches and their treatment of the poor. But that was yesterday. There is similar thinking in many places today. What, we wondered, will tomorrow bring? Are there already seeds of a new order beginning to sprout among the poor? Many believe there are. We had to find out for ourselves and so we turned our attention to the base Christian communities where, we were told, the future's hope could be found. We began to attend base community meetings in Primero de Mayo.

Perceptions of God

During these meetings we discovered a people who rarely thought beyond the needs of the day: getting water, finding work, providing security for themselves and their children. When even these basics were missing from their lives, they believed they were being punished by God for some sin they never understood or had already forgotten.

In meetings, we began to pose the question, "What do you want for your children?" The very idea of such a question was new. People did not "want" or dream or hope. Life was life—you adjusted to it. You did not dream of changing it or even dare dream it might one day be different. As far as anyone knew, life had always been hard, for they believed they were a sinful people and had to be chastized for their offenses by a God who lets nothing escape a rigid sense of justice. This was the God of the conquerors who had destroyed their old gods and condemned their fathers to slavery. Today, this God of the Conquest still rules most of the Mexican poor, keeping order and punishing the slightest deviation from divine eternal law. The poor usually do not know all of God's laws and so they feel they sin often and must be punished, for, whether they knew the law or not, they are responsible for keeping it.

To these poor people, God had been remade into the image and likeness of the local *patron*, or landlord. In rural areas, he held absolute power, rewarding behavior that pleased him and punishing actions that did not. He made no effort to explain his reasons or the correctness of his rules. He was strict, unbending, and often cruel. For the poor, God was no different. God was to be feared and obeyed since God could send punishments more terrible than those imposed by any patron. In the city the patron was replaced by the employer or by the cacique, or political boss. Both had the same absolute power that the poor had already experienced in their patrons.

If God was an angry force, there was still hope, however. More understanding and so more loved was *La Virgen de Guadalupe*, the mysterious mother force who had appeared in Mexico City in 1531, soon after the Conquest. In her Native American garb, speaking a language the poor could understand, she had promised to walk with them in their valley of tears. Even though she could do little to alleviate their suffering, she consoled them in their trials. Her picture was in even the poorest home in Primero de Mayo, for, unlike the God they knew, she understood a mother's pain and a father's discouragement. While God resembled the Native American gods who had demanded human sacrifice and the local patron who ruled peasants' lives with absolute power, La Virgen was more like the old goddess of fertility and joy. She embodied a woman's compassion and a mother's tenderness toward her children. She had described herself as the one who sweeps troubles away.

People were used to bargaining with La Virgen. They promised her flowers if their sick child recovered, or a pilgrimage to a shrine if food could be found, or perhaps to climb her sacred hill in Mexico City on their knees. Once they had made such a promise, it was considered nearly fatal not to fulfill it. Better to make no promises than to make one and then fail to keep it. Even the compassionate Virgen would have to punish that.

This was the residue of Christianity left after 500 years of European domination. It was certainly not a pretty sight. More than the deprivation of water, electricity, and health care, this attitude toward life was destroying the people of Primero de Mayo. Their religion was working hand in glove with the oppressors to keep them passive, accepting the gross injustice with which they lived. Creating a new image of God was the work the sisters had chosen for themselves. With a new idea of God, as One who cares, people in other missions had begun to understand their own dignity and to demand changes in the way they are treated by those with power.[3]

The difference between the poor in Primero de Mayo and the poor in La Nopalera hung on this perception of God. For seven years, the sisters and the people of La Nopalera themselves had struggled to understand the revelation of the Father in Jesus. That catechesis was bearing fruit. People understood that they were the children of a kind and loving God. They sensed that no kind and loving God ever intended people to live without the basics of life. They were in the process of liberating one another from life's most awesome oppression: the belief that things must be as they are and that humankind must always carry the burden of guilt on its shoulders.

It became clear to us that the religion the people of Primero de Mayo lived with was of a pre-Christian sort. Christian words and symbols had been added but at root the oppressive religion of pre-Conquest days was still intact. The Spanish may have built churches, but they never proclaimed the liberating message of Jesus to the poor. Theirs was a technique of domination and control, a cruel parody of Christianity. Bishops, priests, and powerful lay men and women had conspired to distort the message of Jesus to achieve their own ends. There were, of course, exceptions to this—great prophets and heroes—but they were few and their influence marginal.

Commenting on this religion of the conquistadors, the signers of *The Road to Damascus* say:

The God whom the missionaries preached was a God who blessed the powerful, the conquerors, the colonizers. This God demanded resignation in the face of oppression and condemned rebelliousness and insubordination. All that was offered to us by this God was an interior and other-worldly liberation....The Jesus who was preached to us was barely human. He seemed to float above history, above all human problems and conflicts....He condescended to make the poor the objects of his mercy and compassion without sharing their oppression and their struggles. His death had nothing to do with historical conflicts but was a human sacrifice to an angry God.[4]

Liberation

The central message of Jesus—redemption, liberation, salvation— was missing. For the poor, life moved in an endless circle, always the same, always oppressive, always impossible to change. There was a promise that life after death would be better, but even this promise was clouded by a knowledge that one never quite fulfilled the demands of a law that God imposed through the conquerors.

What people today call liberation theology is really no more than a return to the core message of Jesus. He taught that humankind must not be constrained by an idea that God is so intent on conformity to an ideal as to be determined to punish every infraction of divine law. Saint Paul repeated this notion often as he tried to explain that we are freed from the law. This is such a fundamental idea and so profoundly embedded in Euro-American culture that we hardly notice its presence among us. Only when we come upon a whole people who were never given the message of Jesus can we grasp how central to our lives this assumption is.

At different times, believers have expressed this notion in various ways. Some have said that Jesus "saved" humankind from sin. This is a valid summary of the life, death, and resurrection of Jesus—provided we understand the meaning of "saved" and "sin."

We begin with sin since the meaning of saved must depend on our notion of sin. To be saved from drowning is quite different from being saved from ignorance. What is sin? Is it no more than a series of personal infractions of some eternal law? Are these infractions neatly summarized in the Ten Commandments so that all sins begin and end with such actions as misdirected worship, disrespect for those in authority, murder, adultery, theft, false witness, and greed? Even a cursory reading of the Hebrew Scriptures reveals that sin for the Hebrew people was much more. Primarily, it consisted in injustice, since their God was the God of justice and even the acts mentioned by name in the Ten Commandments were acts of injustice.

Injustice shows itself most clearly in the economic and political life of a people. Sin is an unwillingness to recognize the rights of others. To dominate others or to deprive them of their rights as human beings is what the Hebrew people understood by sin, whether this deprivation was focused directly on God or on one's neighbor. Anyone who deprives others of their rights is a sinner. Thus, the military leader who deprives his people of their freedom, the capitalist who deprives his workers of their just wages, or the greedy manufacturer who wastes the world's resources while others go hungry is a sinner, much more of a sinner than the petty thief or the ordinary adulterer.

To be "saved" from such injustice happens in two ways. The oppressor is called from his or her sin by the selfless life of Jesus. The oppressed are endowed with a belief that life does not have to be unjust. They understand that God wills justice, the fair and equal distribution of the goods of this world. Thus they are free to demand change and to insist on the conversion of the sinner. Salvation is a powerful economic and political force. Sin is a determination to maintain the unjust status quo.

To put this another way, as did theologians of an earlier age, we are "redeemed," freed from the kind of slavery that only a misshapen idea of God can impose on us. Since few of us have ever experienced slavery, it is difficult to grasp the force of the word "redemption." It focuses on the price that Jesus paid to break the bonds that held most humans captive to the power of injustice. He stood up against those who had perverted the message of the Father in order to dominate and control the masses. Because of his forceful opposition to those in power, he was tortured and murdered. This was the price Jesus paid for insisting that the Father loved and cared for all human beings and that injustice and oppression, even when clothed in piety, were sin.

Gustavo Gutierrez speaks about the true meaning of salvation:

> If we understand salvation as something with merely "religious" or "spiritual" value for my soul, then it would not have much to contribute to concrete human life. But if salvation is understood as passing from less human conditions to more human conditions, it means that messianism brings about the freedom of captives and the oppressed, and liberates human beings from the slavery that Paul VI referred to. (*Populorum Progressio* n. 47)[5]

To use contemporary terms, we are "liberated" from the awful anxiety that has its origin in the erroneous belief that God is more concerned with order than with justice. Jesus put his revelation in the simplest terms when he taught his disciples to think of God as the father of us all. A father, even in those patriarchal days, wanted the best for his children and cared what happened to them, as the story of the prodigal son has underlined. God sent the prophets to awaken our response to God, not to punish us, but to save us from ourselves and our own greed. God even sent his own son, Jesus, to walk among us and to care deeply about our dignity and to secure our freedom from religious and political oppression, which he was willing to be tortured and killed for.

The Bible's Thrust

Whether our theologizing hangs on notions such as salvation, redemption, or liberation, it must conform to the obvious thrust of the Scriptures or fail to be authentically Christian. No amount of piety can substitute for justice. Jesus' life, death, and resurrection were not focused on religion but on justice. Those who would reduce Christianity to ritual, rules, and the repetition of proper words repeat not the message of Jesus but that of the scribes and Pharisees of Jesus' day.

This is the message we wanted to share with the poor of Primero de Mayo. We wanted them to know that they were God's own children, a people of immense dignity whom no one had the right to oppress or destroy. This message would lead to many insights, as it had earlier in La Nopalera. Most important, it would lead to a sense of dignity and a determination to shake off the oppression that had enslaved them for over 500 years. It began with the question: What do you want for your children? The Bible would have a role to play in answering that question, and the sacraments of the church too, but the first step was at least to ask the question and to admit that one day conditions just might be a little different.

We had begun to see differences among the poor. For those who had grasped the liberating message of Jesus, there was a wonderful freedom and sense of dignity that lifted their spirits immeasurably. Those without this revelation, however, were different; they did not yet have that spirit of the poor that would make them happy. They were very much like so many of the hopeless and depressed poor in the United States who had been taught that only through economic "success" could they be whole. Then the possibility of such success was removed, leaving them with an overpowering sense of guilt and hopelessness. This hopelessness easily led to violence, a violence born of frustration and directed so often at one's fellow poor.

Base Christian Communities

How did a small group of Mexican sisters make such a profound impact on the people of La Nopalera? How had they helped these poor people change their basic perception of God formed through nearly five centuries of servitude? The answer was the base Christian community and a tireless effort at re-evangelizing the poor.

The popular press in North America had introduced the terms "base Christian community" and "liberation theology" to their readers and so we were not surprised to find them in La Nopalera. What did surprise us was the number of communities in one parish, over forty, all meeting weekly to discuss the conditions of their lives in the light of the Bible, and the profound impact these communities have had on the lives of so many people.

We discovered that almost all of our friends in La Nopalera were base community members. Some had been members even before the sisters came to live and work there, but most were recruited and catechized by them.

There is some confusion over what to call this movement that is sweeping Latin America. The most popular name is base Christian community. The word "base" anchors these groups among the poorest, least educated, and often unchurched part of society. This is not another movement for those who are already beginning to put their lives together or who already belong to other church groups. Often those who join a community have had and continue to have no other contact with the church. They are loyal members of a community but do not attend Mass or participate in other church-sponsored activities.

They are, however, definitely Christian for they rely heavily on the teachings of Jesus and on the revelations in the Hebrew Scriptures. They often give fresh interpretations to these ancient texts and think of their lives as parallel to those of the first Christians.

Lastly they are real communities, up-close relationships of men and women who care for one another. They come together to help one another in the often unspoken struggle for justice. They are often the substitute for the extended family structure these people left behind when they immigrated to the city.

The popular term "base Christian community" has aroused

fears in some church leaders. Some of the more conservative believe that the movement is communist or that it threatens clerical authority. For this reason, these leaders have insisted that the groups be called base ecclesial communities to underline the fact that they are a part of the church structure. This term is widely used among the professionals but has little meaning for the ordinary people.

In some areas, Cuernavaca among them, church leaders have frowned on the use of the term "base communities." The people, always willing to avoid unnecessary complications, refer to their groups as "our community" or even as "our reflection group." Whatever the words mean, the reality is that communities of people at the base of church and state are looking hard at life in the light of the Bible. Church and state leaders are terrified at this, for the more independent and liberated the base becomes, the less secure are those who rule them.

One story often told among base community leaders, which we have not yet been able to document, concerns Nelson Rockefeller, then vice president of the United States. After a lengthy visit to Latin America, he is said to have reported that the movement most dangerous to U.S. interests in Latin America was the Base Community Movement and its child, liberation theology.

Another story about the base communities that its leaders like to tell concerns the meeting between a new bishop of Cuernavaca and the base community leaders. He expressed his opposition to base communities and dismissed the whole idea that anything in the church could exist without his permission. One of the leaders, a woman, smiled at the prelate and said, "Your excellency, we respect and love the office of bishop and have read about it in Saint Paul's letters. We also love you, because, like us, you are a child of God and so our brother. We want you to know that we will be patient as we pray for and await your conversion."

These communities are very simple gatherings of poor men and women, usually in the home of one of their members. It is not unusual to see them carrying their own chairs to the meetings since few families have more than one chair for each family member and the communities often have fifteen or twenty members, usually more women than men. Once gathered, the men and women and often older children, too, spend what to North Americans would seem an inordinate amount of time greeting one another and being sure that each person is comfortable in the group.

They then sing one or two long hymns, pray extemporaneously, and settle in for their discussion. There are two slightly different ways to procede. In many parts of Latin America, the discussion begins by relating what is happening in their own lives. They then search the Bible for passages that provide understanding, comfort, or challenge.

In Cuernavaca, however, the discussion begins with a reading from the Bible, usually the gospel of the coming Sunday. It is read twice or even three times since many in the group do not read and cannot easily refer to the text during discussion. The discussion leader then asks the group to repeat what the passage said. The group continues to study the passage itself until each member is sure he or she understands the biblical reality.

Then begins the analysis. The leader usually asks a question such as, "What does this text say to us as individuals and as community?" A long pause follows as people think of what is happening in the community and how this Scripture passage applies. The discussion moves slowly at first and then, when a topic that interests everyone emerges, it develops speed and intensity. The group compares its reality with the biblical reality studied earlier. The hope is that the members will come to a new understanding of their own reality.

Whether the group begins with their own lives and then compares them to the reality in the Bible or begins with the Bible text and then applies it to the reality of their own lives, in either case a confrontation takes place between everyday reality and reality in the Bible.

In both formats the leader then helps the group refocus its attention by asking a question similar to "What is God asking of us as individuals and as community?" followed by "What are we going to do?" When no one has anything else to add, the leader and the group join in prayer and song. In the discussion the group often agrees on some action it will take during the coming week. After the final prayer, the group breaks up slowly with extended goodbyes and expressions of concern for one another.

This is the simple format of groups that have initiated the liberation theology movement, frightened governments around the world, and caused church leaders to take measures to curb their effectiveness. Of this movement Dorothee Solle has written:

> All [of this] is developing in Latin America from a traditional, extremely ritualized Catholicism, which has hardly any preaching, which only celebrates the mass, which traditionally does not engage in any service, but participates in oligarchic rule, and produces no community because it affirms or tolerates as given by nature its main obstacle, the extreme division of society into classes. The renewal of the church in the direction of the kingdom of God which has grown out of the base communities and which is expressed reflectively in liberation theology is one of the great events of church history in our time. In this process, the poor, dispersed, shamed, disorganized people of God is taking part in God's historical liberation.[6]

Our Situation

We had begun to hear the whisper of revelation that was the spirit of the poor, but our search was taking us in unexpected directions, since we believed that economics, politics, history, and theology were no more than different aspects of human life and Jesus spoke to all of them. The notion that Christianity belonged in churches softly wrapped in an odor of incense was the heresy the poor in Latin America had begun to dispel.

There was little doubt in our minds that the profound change in self-understanding taking place at Primero de Mayo would have political consequences both for church and state. Those who had the spirit of the poor were whispering revolution, and the powerful understood their message. The revelation we heard was revolutionary and its time was rapidly approaching.

—Chapter Seven—

Two Base Community Meetings

We attend more and more base Christian communities and come to understand the profound wisdom of these groups of poor and simple people.

In our search for the spirit of the poor, our weekly schedule soon involved attendance at four different base Christian communities, three in La Nopalera and one in the even poorer community of Primero de Mayo. Each is different since the people who attend have vastly different backgrounds. Each Monday evening we attend a community comprised mostly of married couples. Here the dialogue is spirited; the men, especially, apply the Bible readings to the concrete circumstances of their working lives and the women focus on the day-to-day happenings in the community. Both men and women often return to the topic of government injustice in the community and in the workplace.

On Tuesdays at 5:00 we meet with a group that began with mostly women, although four new men have now joined it. On Wednesday afternoons we meet with a group of older women who jokingly say that they are *puras mujeres con Memo*, all women with Bill. Most of these women are widows or have husbands who work in the United States. Lastly, on Saturday evenings we meet with a mixed group in Primero de Mayo.

These experiences defy description or generalizations, so we simply record two of the meetings here. The first took place with the older women's group. The leader, Sister Mari Duran, took a more assertive than normal role so that these women would feel more secure. Several of them do not read or write and some seldom reflect aloud but they do listen and often quote comments that others have made. The topic for the meeting we recorded was the celebration of the important Mexican fiesta, the Day of the Dead.

The second meeting involved our Tuesday group. Josefina, the leader, plays a more passive role, one that is more common in the base communities we have visited. The topic discussed was Jesus' statement, "Render to Caesar the things that are Caesar's and to God the things that are God's."

The Day of the Dead

The origins of the people's most treasured traditions and rituals are shrouded in time. Anthropologists estimate that the land now known as Mexico was flourishing 10,000 years ago. Five hundred years ago, with the Spanish Conquest, new and alien traditions and rituals were introduced and spliced into existing customs. The most notable example of this melding is the apparition of Our Lady of Guadalupe.

Every tradition, every ritual, has multiple interpretations rooted in some far-distant human longing. The people of La Nopalera cannot explain where the traditions came from but are quite determined to preserve them as handed down from their ancestors. The following dialogue from a base community meeting examines one of the people's most cherished traditions, The Day of the Dead, which is actually a novena, nine days, beginning October 24 and ending November 2. The goal of the meeting was to discuss the meaning of the celebration using the methodology of *Ver, Pensar, Actuar* (See, Think about, Act upon).

This gathering of 12 people took place just outside the church door, everyone having brought out a rickety wood and cane chair to form a circle. Besides several children, there were present one baby who nursed from time to time between periods of dozing, the sisters' faithful dog Negro, and three donkeys who hung around the adjacent soccer field and appeared to be listening intently over the stone wall.

After an appropriate hymn and prayer our leader explained the *fruto* (fruit or yield) of the meeting was to understand how and why the Day of the Dead is celebrated, to discuss the difference between the way the rich and the poor celebrate this fiesta, and to help prepare a fiesta that is more open to honoring those who have died because of repression and injustice.

Sister then invited each of us to describe how the Day of the Dead is celebrated in our own community, or in the community we came from.

GLORIA We do many things here in La Nopalera that we did before in our *tierra*. Still, I like to return to my village to celebrate because my relatives died and are buried in the cemetery there. Because our family's lived there so long, we have many rich traditions, like making special foods and placing them on an altar we put in the house, and inviting those who are hungry to eat with us.

PANCHITA I like the celebration we had here in the parish last year because it combined many of the traditions we brought from the places where we were born with some new ideas. I especially liked the crosses we put up on each street with the names of the deceased pinned on them.

BILL This is our first celebration of the fiesta here in Mexico and we are looking forward to being with you. Back in the U.S., some Catholics go to Mass on November 1, the feast of All Saints, and fewer go again the next day, the feast of All Souls. We do put the names of deceased family members in a special place in the church and ask the priests to pray for their souls during the month of November.

PATTY   And the children celebrate Halloween on October 31 by dressing up in costumes and masks and going from house to house asking for treats of candy and fruit.

LUCECITA, LA VIEJITA (who is 84)   I liked the old fiestas, especially all the candles we lit in the cemetery and the beautiful flowers, but I also like the new celebrations the sisters have helped us organize. In the old days we had paths of flower petals from our house to the cemetery and more candles on the graves than you could count.

SISTER MARI   Would some of you comment on how we celebrate this fiesta in the cemeteries?

LUCECITA, LA ABUELITA (Lucy, the grandmother)   Well, we go to the cemetery before sunrise. It's hard to get the little ones ready on time. We take candles, flowers, tools to clean the graves, and some special foods as offerings. We sing and pray and tell stories about the lives of our loved ones who are buried there. We often spend the whole day keeping company with the dead on their special day. We feel very close to them. It's all so beautiful.

(Other members of the group added their reflections on how the fiesta is celebrated in the cemetery and at home.)

SISTER   Now, let's think about why we do all this....Gaby?

GABY   We do this because we want to honor and remember those we love who have died. If we don't have rituals like these, we might get busy with our lives and forget those who have died before us. It's almost like spending a day with my husband and recalling the good times we had together.

BERTA   And I think this is the way we pass on our traditions to our children and grandchildren. Since we have all moved here from other places, it would be easy to leave our traditions and rituals behind and be very sorry later. Children learn that the dead are a part of our families, too.

SISTER   Margarita, how do the rich celebrate the Day of the Dead?

MARGARITA   I can answer that, all right. I used to work for a rich family as a maid. They had a week-long party. Their relatives came from Mexico City to eat and drink day and night. The kids even threw me into the pool once and I can't swim. I was terrified, but most of the people were so drunk they just stood there laughing as I struggled to save myself. On the Day of the Dead they sent me to the cemetery to clean the graves of their relatives and to leave lighted candles. They stayed home for one last festive meal before their guests packed up to go home.

SISTER   Juana, is that any different from the way the poor celebrate?

JUANA   Well, yes. We could never afford to have parties like the rich have and, besides, we poor people want to focus our attention on the dead, to pray, and to remember. This is a sacred time, God's time, not a time to get drunk and act silly.

SISTER   Good. Now everyone, do you think the rich and the poor die as equals?

(A chorus of nos and yeses.)

NORMA   In some ways "no" and in some ways "yes." First, the rich have big, expensive funerals but we poor people have to make real sacrifices just to give our dead a simple but decent burial. But then, the rich and poor do die as equals because the rich can't take their money with them. Besides, the Bible teaches us that we are all equal because we are sons and daughters of God, brothers and sisters.

PATTY   What you're saying reminds me of something from St. Luke's gospel (6:24-25):

But alas for you who are rich:
   you are having your consolation now.
Alas for you who have your fill now:
   you shall go hungry.
Alas for you who laugh now:
   you shall mourn and weep.
(Smiles all around.)

SISTER   In our tradition, we honor many groups of the dead, like who?

BERTA   On October 30, we remember those who have died as children. Other days we honor those who have died of illnesses and accidents. Last year we also honored those who have died as martyrs.

SISTER   Good. Now that we've looked carefully at how we celebrate the fiesta, let's move on to the second part of our process: *Pensar*, to think about. Why do we grieve so for the dead?

PANCHITA   Because we miss them, but we are also happy because they are in heaven with God now and do not suffer as we do in this world.

SISTER   Mago, will you please read 1 Thessalonians 4:13-14 for us?

MAGO   "We want you to be quite certain, brothers and sisters, about those who have died, to make sure that you do not grieve about them, like the other people who have no hope. We believe that Jesus died and rose again, and that it will be the same for those who have died in Jesus: God will bring them with him."

SISTER   Does that make sense to you?

(A chorus of yeses.)

SISTER   Now, even poor people spend lots of money on flowers and food for the Day of the Dead fiesta. Is there something even better we could do to honor the dead?

JUANA   We could work for justice and the coming of God's kingdom.

GABY   Juana's right. Many of our loved ones died because of lack of medical care, because of malnutrition and contaminated water.

NORMA   And what about those who have died as victims of repression, torture, and assassination here in Mexico, in El Salvador, in Guatemala? More than anything, we honor them when we work for justice.

LUCECITA   And God doesn't want us to die prematurely because we are poor and victims of injustice.

SISTER   Jesus says that death comes like a thief in the night and that we have to be prepared. Gloria, will you read Matthew 24:42-44 please?

GLORIA   "So stay awake, because you do not know the day when your master is coming. You may be quite sure of this that if the householder had known at what time of the night the burglar would come, he would have stayed awake and would not have allowed anyone to break through the wall of his house. Therefore, you too must stand ready because the Son of Man is coming at an hour you do not expect."

SISTER   Good. And now let's listen to Jesus' parable of the last judgment where we are judged by our love for the most oppressed. (Matthew 25:31-40)

MAGO   All the things Jesus mentions are things we can do for others if we really care about them.

JUANA   Yes, and the people in the parable are suffering because of injustice and oppression. When we help them, Jesus says, it's the same as doing it for him. I like that a lot.

SISTER   Now that we have followed our process of *Ver* and *Pensar*, what do we still have to consider?

(A chorus of *Actuars*.)

SISTER   Yes, we need to suggest ways to better celebrate the fiesta of the Day of the Dead here in our community.

MAGO   Well, I think we should again put up a cross at the end of each street with the names of the people's loved ones. We'd need a committee to make and decorate those crosses and collect the names.

BERTA   I think we should visit all the families nearby, invite the people to the celebration here at church and at the cemetery, and collect the names of their dead.

LUCECITA   Could we make a large cross to carry to the cemetery at dawn on November 2? We could decorate it and put on it the names of people who have died as victims of injustice.

NORMA   I like that idea. We could include those who died from repression in other Latin American countries.

MEMO   Especially martyrs like Archbishop Oscar Romero, the Jesuits, and the North American women in El Salvador.

GLORIA   And all the catechists and base community leaders who have been murdered.

PANCHITA   And we could add the children that die in Mexico for lack of medicine.

PATTY   And the poor who die slowly of malnutrition in Mexico and throughout the Third World.

MARGARITA   And the poor who die because they do not have hospitals and doctors.

JUANA   All those who have disappeared in Mexico.

GABY   All those who have died from repression throughout Mexico, especially during elections.

SISTER   Very good. Now we can take our suggestions to the base community coordinators' meeting Saturday to help finalize our plans for the celebration of the Day of the Dead. We came together today with three objectives and we've achieved them all using our method of *Ver, Pensar, Actuar*. At our next meeting we'll divide up the work that needs to be done for the fiesta.

Now, let's close with prayers of petition and thanksgiving, recalling especially our loved ones who have died and those who have died from oppression and injustice.

And so the meeting ended.

We were struck by the enthusiasm of the women who talked about this ancient celebration, the European and Mexican roots of which stood so far in the past. These days were at the end of the ancient Celtic year in Europe, and the customs of the Druids had been grafted onto the Christian liturgy centuries before the Spanish conquest of Mexico. The Native Americans, like so many Asians, maintain an intense reverence for their forbearers, and the Day of the Dead incorporated this ancient concern.

It surprised us that the differences between rich and poor were discussed here. They seem to intrude everywhere. Beneath every celebration lies this mystery: why the rich live so differently from their ancestors. In the face of this, the poor are coming to believe that they are the chosen ones of God.

The Problem of Caesar

On another day with a different group we discussed Jesus' pronouncement in the gospel about giving to Caesar what was his and to God what was God's.

The rains that day had not yet begun and the afternoon was oppressively hot, the road dust rising with every breeze as we walked toward Maria's house. Little children were everywhere, some poorly clad, others in rags, and a few younger ones exactly as God had created them. Each one, even the youngest, came up to us to shake our hands with varying degrees of solemnity. Dogs barked nervously but without much enthusiasm, so intense was the heat. We saw many friends looking out their doorways, as they always did those days. We inquired about the sick and about family members who had gone to the U.S. to seek work and often we just waved and smiled a greeting.

As usual we met at 5:00 in the courtyard of Maria's house. We were fourteen adults, eleven women and three men, and all except us were from the same poor neighborhood. In addition, four children played at the edge of the group, a restless dog ambled in and out of the meeting, a dozen chickens clucked around us, and Maria's husband while not a member of the group walked around and listened to what was being said.

Maria's courtyard boasted a gate to the street and several bedrooms opening onto it. A large open space served as a kitchen. We have never been sure just how many people live there, but several people would walk through the yard during our meetings, seeming to be at home.

At precisely five, the family chickens marched up the hill from the river bank where they had spent the day foraging in the garbage-strewn ravine. The rooster noisily herded his family of hens and chicks into the enclosure of the courtyard where bits of corn were spread on the ground for them. Since they arrived about the same time we did, we had gotten to know them, thinking of them as a part of the community. Here in La Nopalera all God's creatures lived together and shared what they had.

The text we read was the story of the pharisees' and Herodians' attempt to trap Jesus by asking him whether it was lawful to pay tribute to Caesar or not (Matthew 22:15-22). Jesus' response was simple enough. He looked at the coin and asked whose image was on it. When his adversaries replied that it was Caesar's, he told them to render to Caesar what was Caesar's and to God what was God's.

After reading the passage twice and pausing while some individuals struggled to find the passage in their Bibles, our discussion went like this:

JOSEFINA (the leader)   What does this say about our lives here in the community?

MARTA   Well, it talks about paying taxes and we do a lot of that. It sounds like it says that it is all right to pay taxes. The people back then must have wondered if they should.

CARMEN   It tells us that we should stay out of politics and just give the government what it deserves and the church what it deserves. We ought to pray a lot and stay out of things like fighting for water and electricity. I've been going to one of the new sects and that's what they teach there. The minister tells us we should pray and obey the commandments and leave running the country to the government.

FERNANDO   Well, I was thinking about the taxes, too. I know I have to pay them even when I don't want to, but what's the government supposed to do in return? We pay our taxes and they're supposed to give us something back. It's like going to a store. You pay the storekeeper and she gives you some merchandise. If she doesn't, she's cheating you.

JOSEFINA   But that's what happens to us. We get nothing in return for our taxes. We don't get water part of the time and we are never sure of the electricity. The children are not getting a decent education and the police won't help you at all unless you bribe them. We pay our taxes and get nothing in return, or almost nothing.

CARMEN   There we go making something political out of a Bible passage that isn't political at all. I think it says that we should pay our taxes and then pray to God that they won't go up, and that the government will do right by us. Prayer is all you need to solve all problems. That's what the Bible teaches.

LUPE   I don't think the government will treat us with respect and justice unless we demand that they do. We have to pay our taxes and then demand that they be used for things like water, electricity, schools, and police protection. Our demands are the only things that will make them honest and just.

JUANA   But isn't this political? You're talking about marches, petitions, and demonstrations. Jesus doesn't talk about that kind of thing; he's interested in prayer and growing closer to God by living a good life without sin.

MEMO   I think I remember a time when Jesus marched in a political demonstration.

LUZ   You do? When was that? Wait a minute. It was Palm Sunday, wasn't it? Jesus rode the donkey and the people all marched with him to the Temple. It was a demonstration against the injustice of the scribes and Pharisees. Well, Juana, what about that?

JUANA   Yes, he did march. He was political, wasn't he? But that doesn't mean we don't have to pray. Prayer is the most important thing we do.

MAGO   Prayer is important for me, but so is trying to make life a little better for my children. Many days I don't have enough to feed them and when they get sick I can't afford to pay for the doctor. That's not right. I would rather use the tax money to feed my children because the government gives us nothing in return for our money.

LUPE   The reason it doesn't give us anything is that we don't demand it. Remember when they shut off the water to the colonia and we sent a delegation to find out why. They said that the former administrator had not paid the electric bill and so the pump was turned off. We were supposed to suffer for his sins. When we showed how angry we were, they changed their tune and restored the water. If we don't complain, we get nothing. Jesus says that we should pay our taxes, but I think he must mean that we have to keep the pressure on the government to use the taxes for a good purpose, too.

ISABEL   When we don't say anything, the government thinks we don't care. Then the officials just spend the money on themselves and we get nothing. We have to organize ourselves and make them respect us. It isn't easy to be poor.

ARNULFO   I agree, the government has a responsibility to us. But what about the church? We have to pay in church, too.

JOSEFINA   We don't pay much at the church, but you're right, the church does have a responsibility to us, just as the government does. The sisters use every peso for the buildings and for helping the sick. They show the parish committee where every centavo goes. They even invite us to suggest what we think should be done. Getting that room for a clinic is an example of a suggestion someone made. They account for everything, unlike our government.

PATTY   What about the priests, the bishop, and the pope? Are they doing what they should?

ALICIA   Who knows? We never see them except for some official event when they come and go so fast no one can really talk with them.

MARTA   I guess that's true of the bishop. The two priests who come to say Mass every third week are good men. They listen, but what can they do? They are almost as poor as we are.

JOSEFINA   The bishop seems very nice, but he yells when he speaks and this frightens many people.

LUZ   He also makes fun of the children when they can't answer his questions. I feel embarrassed because I can't answer them either. I wonder why he doesn't send us a priest to have

Mass every Sunday the way they do in rich people's churches?

MARIA   That's the way it always is; the rich get what they want and we don't.

JOSEFINA   This time we might be better off. We have the sisters and they really care about us. They visit the sick, have funerals, catechize the children, start our communities, lead the Sunday celebrations, and help us manage our parish money—and they never ask us for a peso. The only thing they don't do is say Mass.

ISABEL   Then why doesn't the bishop let them say Mass for us?

ARNULFO   He can't do that. They aren't priests, and you have to be a man and unmarried to be a priest.

ISABEL   Who says so?

DELIA   The pope says so. Anyway, we're better off than the people at Tres Pollos who got a priest last year. All he does is fight with the communities. He wants to be in charge of everything; he makes fun of the people and calls their children stupid. He wants money for everything he does. I'd rather have the sisters than a priest like that.

FERNANDO   I agree, but I really don't see why one of them can't say Mass. They're good women who care about the gospel and care about us. I think we should demand a change.

MEMO   We have talked about the government and the church. What about God? Does God have any responsibilities toward us?

MARIA   That's a strange question....I'm not sure we should talk about God that way.

FERNANDO   No, it's a good question. I think God does have responsibilities toward us. God is our father and fathers have responsibility. God has the responsibility of loving us and taking care of us. That's what it means to be a father.

MARTA   God acts in a responsible way to us, trying to get close to us and to care for us. When God can't, it's our fault. We get so busy that we don't have time for God.

MEMO   I apologize if my question seemed irreverent. I didn't mean it that way. All I wanted to say is that we have to tell the government and the church what we need. We have to keep the pressure on them all the time. I was thinking that we have to do the same thing with God and that's what we call prayer.

JUANA   Ah, that's much better. I see what you mean. We have to pray always, always tell God what we need.

FERNANDO   But we have to keep the pressure on the government and the church. We have to be political and prayerful at the same time.

PATTY   I remember that Saint Benedict had a motto: Pray and work. I guess that could be our motto, too.

JOSEFINA   Let's make all this practical. What can we do?

JUANA   We can start by praying more, praying all the time.

ISABEL   Yes, and what else?

MAGO   What about joining the group that's protesting the big increase in our water bills. My bill went from eight thousand to nineteen thousand pesos in two months.

FERNANDO   Yes, let's do that. Some of the families with children are going to have their water turned off because they can't pay the new rates.

ROSA   Some of the old people, too. Some of the grandmothers are already carrying buckets of water from the church because they can't afford to pay. Maybe we can make a difference.

LUZ   I'll talk to a friend who is on the committee and see how we can help if everyone wants me to.

(A chorus of agreement.)

JOSEFINA   Let's pray then...

God of the poor, hear our prayers today. We are your children and we need you in our daily lives. You love the poor and understand us when we call to you, and so we say...Our Father....

The meeting closed with a popular song:

When the poor believe in the poor,
    we are able to sing of liberty.
When the poor believe in the poor,

we will build true fraternity.
When the poor look to the poor
and begin to organize,
then our liberation begins.
When the poor speak to the poor
of the hope which God has given us,
the kingdom of God is born among us.

The meeting ended but the conversation lingered on. By this time the noisy chickens had gone to roost and the excited dog was lying contentedly in a corner of the yard. Maria's husband had left the house for more interesting company. We began to drift to the street where the children greeted us. Together we went to look at the new tar-paper shack Rosa and her new husband, Fernando, had just constructed.

Rosa is sixty and her husband looks much older. He is a widower and she a widow. They had claimed a steep section on the embankment leading to the river, a section of land no one really wanted because of the danger of mud slides during the rainy season and the stench of raw sewage in the stream below. There the two of them lashed poles together and covered them with pieces of corrugated tar-paper. There was no electricity, no water, and no plumbing, but it was home for these newlyweds. It was all they had.

As we walked to the bus stop accompanied by our friends, we wondered if this community was not like the ones to whom Saint Paul wrote so many years ago. One thing was sure, the Spirit of God had filled their hearts and in time they, more than the rest of us, would renew the face of the earth.

Chapter Eight

Celebrating Reality: The Fiesta of Our Lady of Guadalupe

We celebrate the Fiesta of Our Lady of Guadalupe with our friends at La Nopalera and discover insights into their character and culture.

Celebration

The movies about Mexico we saw as children always had a fiesta scene: men, women, and children dancing and singing with great abandon. In our first year at La Nopalera we had not seen a real fiesta. There were celebrations of First Communion, confirmation, baptism, weddings, and the *Quinceanos* celebrations of 15-year-old girls, but never a fiesta of a whole community. There were, of course, secular holidays, many of them, but they never captured the popular imagination. We wondered if the drudgery of modern life had destroyed the poor's love of celebration. Perhaps, we thought, celebration might no longer be part of the spirit of the poor.

That was before we participated in the Fiesta of Our Lady of Guadalupe and its extension through Christmas and Epiphany. The fiesta recalls that the Virgin Mary appeared to a poor Native American, Juan Diego, in 1531, shortly after the Conquest. The appearance took place on a small hill called Tepeyac, then outside Mexico City but now well within the city's urban sprawl. The hill itself was sacred to an Aztec goddess, Tecoatlasupe. She was known both as a goddess of fertility and as the one who banishes all evil. Mary spoke in Juan Diego's native tongue, was clothed in native dress clearly marked with Native American symbols, and had about her waist the typical cincture worn by pregnant women. Thus, the apparition of Mary was easily understood and accepted by the poor and powerless Native Americans.

As proof to the bishop who would not believe Juan Diego's story, Mary sent a bouquet of roses wrapped in Juan Diego's serape and when he presented them to the bishop, the roses fell to the floor revealing the image of the mysterious woman, which is, after more than 450 years, intact and on display at the shrine of Our Lady of Guadalupe in Mexico City.

Mary promised to be with the poor during the suffering that was to follow. From the arrival of the Europeans until the end of the 1500s, the population dropped from nearly 24,000,000 to about 900,000, as we have seen. This period following the European conquest introduced a slavery comparable to that in the Soviet Union during the darkest days of Stalin's reign. Bartholomé de Las Casas, writing about this time, described conditions in Cuba that were common throughout the Spanish Empire.

The men were sent out to the mines, as far as [250 miles away], while their wives remained to work the soil, not with hoes or plowshares drawn by oxen, but with their own sweat and sharpened poles....Thus husbands and wives were together only once every eight or ten months and when they met they were so exhausted and depressed on both sides that they had no mind for marital communication and in this way they ceased to procreate. As for the newly born, they died early because their mothers, overworked and famished, had no milk to nurse them, and for this reason, while I was in Cuba, 7000 children died in three months. Some mothers even drowned their babies from sheer desperation, while others caused themselves to abort with certain herbs that produced stillborn children.[1]

The Native Americans who survived had a profound devotion to La Virgen, as they call her. She, they believed, was on their side in their struggle to remain alive. She was their champion, and when Mexico first fought for its independence from Spain, her picture adorned their flags. Her solidarity with the poor and powerless was what the fiesta celebrated then and is what is still celebrated by the poor today.

As one might expect, not all Mexicans celebrate the Feast of Our Lady of Guadalupe as a hope for justice and a challenge to the established order. For nearly five centuries, those in power have attempted to blunt the apparition's demand for justice: The original name of the apparition was changed from Tecoatlasupe to the Spanish Guadalupe, the miraculous image was crowned with jewels to identify her with the world's rich and powerful, and Mary was presented as the ideal of totally passive womanhood. Every effort was made by authorities in both church and state to tame the hope for change the indigenous poor people saw and still see in the ancient story.

Experiencing the Feast Day

During the days leading up to December 12, the feast day itself, we saw ever-increasing activity around the church and heard reports that there would be mariachi and other kinds of music, a procession, and dancing at the church followed by fiestas in the streets. Although ready for a special treat, we were not sure what the celebration would entail.

We were not disappointed; the reality surpassed our fondest

dreams. This rag-tag community of poor people put together what can only be called an extravaganza. On Sunday afternoon, December 10, as we waited outside the church in La Nopalera to greet our friends, we heard the sound of a very brassy band in the distance and saw a group of campesinos marching in our direction, stirring up the ever-present dust. They played every kind of bent, dented, and homemade instrument and were followed by a throng of people carrying flowers and singing with gusto. In the middle of the commotion came the picture of Our Lady of Guadalupe, held high by several of our friends from Primero de Mayo.

Right up the street, through the gates and into the church marched the procession. They were greeted by the sisters who received Our Lady's picture and placed it in front of the altar. We stood in awe as the crowd swelled and swelled while the band retreated into the distance, playing what we came to recognize as the Guadalupana Song.

So began a swirl of activities. The next afternoon at the church in La Nopalera we found people on ladders putting up garlands of paper flowers. Others were stringing up a canopy of flour sacks in front of the church to provide shade for performers the following day. We were immediately put to work hauling stones to make an outdoor grotto for the large picture of Our Lady of Guadalupe, which would preside over all the festivities.

The area around the church was busy with activity. Children raced about with the sisters' dog Negro, while the adults rushed to complete their decorating before nightfall. Then, magically, the dull, dusty churchyard, lighted by bulbs hung from the bougainvilleas, was transformed into a carnival of color. We quickly hauled the chairs and benches out of the church into the yard. Ladders were stored, and homemade brooms whisked away any trash left about. It had come together just in time for all of us to walk about a mile down the steep, winding road to _Los Pinos_, where the festivities officially began.

Mariachi music was in the air as people stepped out into the streets to join us, carrying flowers and lighted candles. Because of the cool December air, many wore sweaters or shawls. Soon we were a crowd of 300, from babies to old women and men, and the crowd kept growing.

With candles glowing and with the picture of Our Lady of Guadalupe held high in our midst, we retraced our route to La Nopalera. The mariachi band led the way as firecrackers burst overhead. Dogs barked, children ran about, and roosters crowed as we processed toward La Nopalera.

As we turned the corner to the church, there were what looked like large animals dancing in front of the mariachi band. These dancing animals now led the procession, which by now numbered over a thousand people. We skirted the crowd and came up alongside the ingeniously costumed dancers, many of whom wore costumes of animals while others were dressed as campesinos. All, large and small, were heading into the church yard performing a ritualized dance which, we later learned, emulates the plumed serpent, sacred to the ancient peoples of Mexico.

We stood mesmerized by the spectacle of the dancers leading the procession, followed by the mariachi and over a thousand people carrying candles and singing. In the darkness we spotted another even stranger looking group of dancers. They all wore the same mask: a dark face with a huge and fanciful beard. On their heads was what looked like large lampshades turned upside down and draped with imitation pearls, jewels, and other gaudy decorations. What a sight these dancers were, twirling in a circle and stirring up dust, their full-length gowns of bright satin held out at breast level in a rather lascivious looking gesture. These were Chanelos, performing a popular dance of Central Mexico.

Later, we heard several versions of the history of the dance of the Chanelos. Some say the dance originated in the time of the Moorish Conquest of Spain and makes fun of the Moors. Others think it originated among the poor in Mexico to ridicule the Spanish overlords. The dance is particularly popular in the festivities leading up to Mardi Gras. Some groups of Chanelos dancers spend all year preparing their costumes for these performances.

Somehow, the crowd sorted out as people placed flowers and candles in front of the statue of Our Lady in the grotto we had built that afternoon. Our Lady of Guadalupe, the mother of the Mexican people, looked down on her children as we sang and clapped and celebrated through the evening. We had never experienced anything like it; we were overwhelmed and filled with gratitude that we could be with our friends and begin to grasp how important Our Lady is in the life of the people, especially the poor.

About 11 P.M., Julia and Hermilo with whom we planned to spend the night told us it was time to go to their house to prepare for the street celebration. After our usual hugs and good nights, we picked up our bags and headed down the hillside to their home. Some people stayed behind to keep vigil with Our Lady through the night. They were beginning to wrap themselves in their _rebosos_, or scarves, and heavy sweaters.

Street Celebrations

It seemed that everyone in La Nopalera was celebrating in the streets, which were decorated with garlands and Christmas lights. People greeted us from their doorways. There was music and the crack of fireworks in the crisp air.

Nothing is hurried in La Nopalera, so it was nearly 2:00 A.M. before the men brought small tables and chairs into the street and the women followed with huge steaming pots of food and hot punch. Soon we had joined tables and could seat about 50 people. All the families shared their food. Some of the teenagers brought a boom box and music blared as the younger children, still going strong, played and helped build a bonfire to warm us. Meanwhile, other celebrations were going on in nearby streets as we ate, set off more fireworks, danced, or gathered closer to the bonfire.

About 5:00 A.M., back at Julia and Hermilo's, we heard a sound that we immediately recognized as the brass band from Primero de Mayo. They had played all night. As we prepared for a couple of hours sleep, Julia announced the day's events at the church.

"First," she said, "the sisters want you to come for breakfast. Later in the morning, the Chinelos will dance in front of Our Lady, and in the afternoon the animal dancers will present a story in dance, performing on ropes above where we sit."

"Then," added 12-year-old Veronica, "our youth group is going to perform a socio-drama after Mass at 5:00 P.M."

More Celebrations

When we arrived at the church, people sat around sipping hot punch which was immediately offered to us. Women who lived nearby continued to bring more in large pots. The vigil-keepers still sat in front of Our Lady, tightly wrapped from the cold night air. How could they sit there all night? we wondered.

The sisters greeted us at their house, served breakfast, and asked us about our evening with the Reynoso family. They were amused when we told them we were still dancing at 3:30 in the morning. They sensed how much staying the night in La Nopalera meant to us and rejoiced at our obvious enjoyment.

"There's lots more to come," said Sister Tonya. "You're planning to stay, aren't you?"

"Of course," Bill replied. "We wouldn't miss a minute of this extraordinary feast."

So we settled in for the day, and watched as little children, dressed as Indian maidens or as Juan Diego, the man to whom Our Lady appeared at Tepeyac, came with their parents, brothers and sisters, and grandparents. The crowd swelled as the dancers performed for Our Lady, twirling in their costumes to the tempo of the Chinelo music. The children in the audience who watched off to the side tried to imitate them.

Early in the afternoon, we heard a whistle and drum as the animal dancers made their grand entrance into the church yard and up to the grotto of Our Lady, bowing in a gesture of homage. We spotted Rico's brothers, the youngest of whom was wearing deer antlers on his head.

Sister Mari Lopez, who was sitting with us, told us that the entire dance troupe of 24 young men was from one large family who brought the tradition of the dance with them when they moved from the state of Guerrero. The grandfather, who was busy securing ropes from the church roof to a tree, had trained and directed the dancers. "No one knows how old these dances are, or the stories they will act out," Sister continued as she pointed to the ropes above our heads.

We couldn't believe our eyes as the dancers climbed up onto the flimsy ropes and stalked from one end to the other, pausing to flip over and return to standing positions. To the beat of the whistle and drum, they acted out an ancient tale of hunters and a dog pursuing a tiger through a forest.

The huge crowd sat mesmerized as the drama unfolded during the next hour. The children cheered and shouted to the performers, calling to the tiger to elude the hunters, which it finally did. After the drama on the ropes above us, as if that were not enough, the indefatigable dancers repeated their undulating dance of the plumed serpent before backing out of the church yard, continuing to pay homage to Our Lady. These poor young men practice for months before the feast of Guadalupe and perform only for that event each year.

A Short Break

After lunch at Julia and Hermilo's house where the animal dancers joined us, we returned to the church yard which was filled with people carrying flowers and shepherding costumed children. In spite of the weeks of preparation and a grueling two days of celebration, everyone was still energetic and took part in the closing liturgy with enthusiasm. Looking at the statue of Our Lady of Guadalupe, one might have thought of Mary saying, "Well done, children. Once again you have shown how much you love me."

As the sun set, we streamed up to receive communion. Behind the church, the mountains took on their nighttime purple, and night settled upon this poor community of Christians. At that moment, in that place, God seemed close at hand. What more could we ask than to be with these people covered with a canopy of love?

The Spirit of the Poor

After some rest, we were ready to analyze what participation in that fiesta meant to us, what it might have revealed about these poor people and about their spirit. It was clear that the sisters and the planning committee had cleverly woven together the ancient customs of the people of La Nopalera with the stories of the apparition of Our Lady of Guadalupe and the introduction of Christianity. How beautifully they had merged the myths, symbols, and customs to project the true meaning of the celebration. But what did all this reveal about "the spirit of the poor"?

Had we not had two encounters with North Americans about the same time, we might have missed one of the feast's most important insights. The first encounter was with a well-educated, younger, middle-aged North American who had worked for over ten years with the Latin American poor. He was an admirable person who loved to play with children and often rescued families from financial disaster with his own meager funds. He lived in a poor neighborhood to be closer to the people, and since he was not a priest or a religious, he had no institutional security should he become ill or disabled. He was a model for today's missionary.

One day he showed us a booklet in Spanish that attempted to debunk the Guadalupe story. It was directed to the more "educated" and skeptical Mexican people, those who were ashamed of the popular piety of the poor and, they believed, gullible people. It followed the usual line of reasoning, searching for inconsistencies in the nearly 500-year-old story and seemed to find them.

We read the booklet and listened as the man cast doubt on the historical facts of the apparition. He was sincere; he had been trained to look for absolute accuracy in historical events. In the Guadalupe story there are historical inaccuracies. Yet, we sensed that having this information made him feel superior to the poor, uneducated, and seemingly misled Mexican people. He had professional knowledge that set him apart, or so it seemed.

Fortunately, we had read enough "scientific" information that seemed to buttress the authenticity of the ancient story. But that was not the important thing. Whether or not the apparition had taken place exactly as claimed, whether or not it could be historically validated, it embodied what was pivotal to the whole outlook of the poor: God's concern for the powerless and Mary's promise to mother her most neglected children.

The Guadalupe story is more than a story about an event almost 500 years ago. It is a promise in which the poor find reason to hope, a sign of God's concern for them and, thus, of their dignity as a people. To destroy or make fun of the story and the people's faith in it was to superciliously mock the soul of the poor and their hope for a better world.

Our North American friend and many other learned people do not understand that the poor learn through traditional stories and treasure them for reasons much deeper than their historical accuracy. They are not, at bottom, really interested in whether the events in the story "actually happened" or not. The question does not arise in their minds. The story is accepted from their heritage as is. The attempt to destroy the myths of the poor may be the cruelest imperialism the rich and powerful have yet devised.

Robert Bly has this to say in *Iron John*, his book about masculine growth:

We are each on the way from the Law to the Legends, from dogma to the Midrash, from the overly obedient man to wildness....The closer a person comes to the Legends, then the closer he or she comes to depth, moistness, spontaneity and shagginess....How does this motion begin? The writer and analyst say that when a man is ready to make a decisive move toward "The Legends" a feminine figure whose face looks both ways may appear in his dreams. It is as if she has two faces: one looks toward the world of rule and laws, and the other toward the world of dragonish desire, moistness, wildness, adult manhood. This dream figure is not a flesh and blood woman but a luminous eternal figure.[2]

What is true in the growth of individuals is also true for groups of people. Our Lady of Guadalupe is very much the feminine figure who looks both ways: toward the Spanish preoccupation with dogma, rules, structures of authority and the rational, and toward the Native American desire for legends, stories, consensus, and the mystical. As the poor view the image of Guadalupe, they are caught up in conflict between the two realities but one that confers on them an identity as lovers of the woman they do not yet understand but sense is at their side. Perhaps this is the deeper meaning of the *mestizo* culture that Mexicans prize so deeply, to be realists and yet mystics, to be deeply religious and yet to live with a certain skepticism toward all things religious.

The Mexican poor do believe in Our Lady of Guadalupe, that Mary revealed herself to Juan Diego, and because they do, they understand that Mary is not only at their side but on their side in their struggle to win justice from a reluctant world. The presence of Mary among them has given them a sense of importance, a dignity that no abstract, universal teaching could have achieved. Encyclicals, theological tracts, elaborate liturgies, and closely-reasoned texts may reach the well educated and the professionals, but it is stories that reach directly into the hearts of the poor, and the most powerful religious story in Mexico is the tale of Mary and the uneducated Native American, Juan Diego.

Contrasting our modern, secular attitude toward belief and the whole area of the sacred, Mircea Eliade, the historian of religions, writes:

> For modern consciousness, a physiological act—eating, sex, and so on—is in sum only an organic phenomenon, however much it may still be encumbered by taboos....But for the

primitive such an act is never simply physiological; it is, or can become, a sacrament, that is, a communion with the sacred....[3]

The second of our encounters was with a North American woman, a person dedicated to changing the perception of women in modern life. We agreed with many of her concerns, for it is obvious by now that women have been under-appreciated and oppressed through the centuries. Yet, it was a chance remark she made that helped us understand how far removed she was from the simple faith of the people with whom we had celebrated in La Nopalera.

A group of us were talking about Mary one day over lunch. She asserted at one point, "I can never accept devotion to Mary again. She has been used to manipulate us women and to create an image that all women should remain passive, no matter what happens in their lives."

Considering the oppression of women over such a long period, perhaps her anger should have been directed at society in general or possibly at the church, but why at Mary? How different was her perception of Mary from that of the women in the base communities of La Nopalera or even from that of the Benedictine sisters who lead the community. They see Mary not as a passive woman but as a prophet who demands the rights of the poor and the hungry, a powerful force for change in their world.

We had seen this understanding of Mary in so many of the celebrations in La Nopalera. She was held up as the model of the person concerned for the community. Not only did she comfort the suffering, she challenged the system that made them suffer. Her voice was the voice of the powerless demanding justice. She promised that God would put down the princes of power from their thrones and exalt the lowly. She assured us that the hungry would be fed while the rich would be sent away empty. She provoked the miracle at Cana for a poor and embarrassed couple and thus set in motion the public life of Jesus. She had the courage to stand at the foot of the cross beside her son when Peter and the others had gone into hiding.

Perhaps this difference in understanding Mary has its roots in our different origins. By and large, North Americans are a European people while the Native Americans of Mexico are descended from Asians. Bly says:

In her ability to get the plot of life moving, the Woman...resembles the Hindu feminine, the Shakti, more than the Western feminine, whom custom imagines as receptive and passive. Shakti, whom we see in many Indian paintings, is erect, instigating, up-leaping, fiery, outrageous. In some paintings Shiva (the masculine) lies nearby on the ground or even under her feet, apparently asleep; he is by contrast receptive, cool, laid back, deeply inside himself.

The relations of this instigating woman to Mary Magdalene bears looking at. Her impulse to cause trouble, throw the spark into the dry wood, pull energy out of the stagnant psyche, stir the sea with a single hair, deserves some study and some notice.[4]

It is no accident that John's gospel presents Mary as the one who instigated the public ministry of Jesus at the wedding feast of Cana. Nor should it be lost on us that her reason for provoking his public life was a poor couple who could not entertain their guests properly. It was she, then, who was and is the instigating woman who loves the poor. She is also, of course, the woman who looks both ways, into the old Hebrew culture and into our own. In her all is one.

Pope John Paul II, surely no feminist, seemed to understand something of this crusading zeal of Mary when in a homily at Zapoplan, a poor area in Mexico, he said:

In her Magnificat (Luke 1:46-55), Mary proclaims that God's salvation has to do with justice for the poor. From her, too, stems authentic commitment to other human beings, our brothers and sisters, especially to the poorest and neediest and to the necessary transformation of society.[5]

The spirit of the poor, at least of the Catholic poor, treasures the role of Mary. They endlessly repeat her stories and celebrate her concern for the community of the poor. She is one of them in a very real way, not because she passively accepted suffering but because she demanded justice and stood in the long line of male and female prophets of the Old Testament.

Earlier the North American feminist had told us that the average family in her area needed $75,000 a year to live a reasonably comfortable life. Most of our friends in La Nopalera live on less than $3,000 a year and raise large families on this small amount. Some, especially the older women, have no visible means of support and survive on the generosity of their poor neighbors. We noticed the contrast between this North American woman and her anger with Mary, on the one hand, and, on the other, the simple happiness and joy of the poor of La Nopalera.

Once more we understood that the spirit of the poor brought happiness and the spirit of the rich bred frustration and conflict. Thanks to the chance remarks of our North American friends, we were plunging deeper into the mystery that is the spirit of the poor.

In that spirit there is room for celebration, for unaffected joy, for hope in the future, for Mary, and for a belief in the providence of God, a belief that encourages active struggle against the powers of evil that dominate their world.

—Chapter Nine—

Rediscovering the Incarnation: Christmas to Epiphany

Living with the poor puts us in touch with some of the most profound truths celebrated in the Christmas liturgy.

During the Feast of Our Lady of Guadalupe, we had learned that the art of celebration was well practiced among the poor in La No-palera and Primero de Mayo. The feast had taught us the importance of celebration to ward off despair. We had watched as one generation shared its deepest hopes with the next and imparted to them a sense of inner dignity. The feast had taught us that the poorest of the poor have a sense of their own worth and that this is reinforced by their simple celebrations.

Now we wondered what revelations the Christmas season would bring. Would we find the same enthusiasm for the stories of Christmas that we had experienced during the Guadalupan feast? What insights into the meaning of the spirit of the poor would Christmas bring?

Posadas and Piñatas

The answer to our questions came sooner than expected, for on December 17 the people began to celebrate the *posada* season, an ancient Spanish tradition taught by the missionaries centuries earlier. Their ancestors had practiced it faithfully in their mountain villages, even when there were no priests, no sacraments—and no interest by the official church in these poor people.

Each evening, groups of people gathered at the church doors in La Nopalera and processed, singing, to the house of one of their neighbors, where they reenacted a ritual dialogue in song. Standing outside the house, part of the group asked if Mary and Joseph could come in, since she was weary and ready to give birth to a child. The other part of the group answered in song, "No, we have no room." After several verses of singing back and forth, Mary and Joseph were finally given shelter and the host family invited everyone inside to celebrate.

The celebrations were simple enough. Adults shared punch and a little food if the host family could afford it. Then they brought out a piñata, a large clay container decorated with colorful paper and filled with peanuts and fruit. The piñata was hung in the yard above the crowd and blindfolded children took turns striking at it with a stick or pipe until, hitting it at last, it broke open, its contents spilling to the ground where the children dove into the pile to grab what peanuts and fruit they could. Each evening just after dark, the drama was repeated at a different home. In a very simple way, children and adults were learning that when they accept powerless and neglected people into their lives they are welcoming Jesus, Mary, and Joseph.

During the posada season we began to realize that Jesus, Mary, and Joseph are as real and present to these struggling people as are their families or neighbors; they are models for their lives. Adults and children unselfconsciously speak of them not as part of an ancient myth far removed from daily life, but as present here and now.

As the posadas went on and Christmas drew nearer, we felt

closer to the Christmas event than we had ever felt before. Perhaps it was the setting: the people of La Nopalera were as poor as Mary and Joseph must have been, the land as dry, with dust covering everything, as in ancient Palestine. Donkeys, mules, and horses roamed the streets. There were no malls or gifts from Santa Claus. The biggest influence on us, however, was the people's spirit as they anticipated the birth of the baby Jesus. Not distracted by shopping for gifts, they focused on the Christmas story which seemed to be happening again in their midst. It was easy to imagine themselves seeking shelter while traveling or giving birth to a child in a stable. Their lives made Christmas real and they believed that this child, God's son, came into the world to proclaim the "good news" to them.

This season held a special excitement for the children. It was their Santa Claus, Christmas tree, gifts, and parties all rolled into one. Yet, they were absorbing more than fruit and candy. They were learning to see the world in a way different from our own. We knew this from the expressions on their faces and chance remarks they made, but we did not fully understand it. We went rushing back to our tattered copy of Eliade's *The Secular and the Sacred*, looking for some confirmation of what we thought we had discovered.

> What we find as soon as we place ourselves in the perspective of [the religious person] of the archaic societies is that the world exists because it was created by the gods, and that the existence of the world itself "means" something, wants to say something, that the world is neither mute nor opaque, that it is not an inert thing without purpose or significance. For the religious [person], the cosmos lives and speaks. The mere life of the cosmos is proof of its sanctity, since the cosmos was created by the gods and the gods show themselves to [people] through cosmic life.[1]

The people of La Nopalera had that ability to see the hand of

God in everything, in the beauties of nature, the long and sometimes painful dry season, the often terrifying thunderstorms, illness, and even death. God is present to them. Their lives, like the
rest of the cosmos, have meaning, and since the world is ultimately God's, not theirs, they try to live in gentle harmony with it and
with one another. Here was the simple message of the posadas:
living in harmony with everyone, even the stranger, because we
are all one human family living in a single home, the universe
God provided for us.

Room for Us at the Inn

Never had we looked forward to Christmas as we did that year,
even though we were far from our family in the United States and
Brazil. When Julia, our ever-sensitive friend, asked us what we
were planning to do for Christmas, we replied that our only plan
was to be with the people of La Nopalera on Christmas Eve.

"Then, you must stay with us," she stated emphatically. "We
have your bed ready. We will go to Mass at 9:00 that evening and
then have a street fiesta as we did for Our Lady of Guadalupe."

We made half-hearted protests that we would be imposing by
taking their bed, but her husband, Hermilo, brushed them aside.
"But Christmas is the time to be with family and we don't want
you to be alone. You must spend Christmas with us."

Even though our conditions were somewhat different from
those of Mary and Joseph, we experienced the same feeling of
welcome they must have, the welcome the poor always extend to
strangers. We realized how badly we had misunderstood Luke's
words, "She wrapped him in swaddling clothes and laid him in a
manger because there was no room for them at the inn" (Luke
2:7). While there may have been no room at the local inn, some
unknown family welcomed Mary and Joseph into their home and
provided her with the best place available to have her child.
Women must have rushed into the little stable to help at the birth
while men stood by, waiting anxiously, as they often do at times
like that. Far from being alone in a strange land, Joseph and Mary

were with other caring people. They were part of the community of the poor, and on that Christmas Eve so were we.

We arrived at the church as Sister Fidelina was ringing the heavy bell. Bundled against the evening chill, families streamed into the church. As for La Virgen, flowers were everywhere and a large manger scene stood to one side of the altar. We greeted our friends and sat down. The Mass began with joyful singing.

There was no holding back; everyone entered into the spirit of this special night. We were swept up into the liturgy, which ended with everyone walking in procession to the altar to kiss a statue of the baby Jesus. Some older people had tears in their eyes as they approached the statue, remembering happier Christmases perhaps or children who had died. Children kissed the statue shyly. Every age brought a different set of memories to the moment, but all were immersed in a simple piety that made Jesus seem so real that he became part of their community.

We spent the next half-hour giving and receiving Christmas greetings outside the church before returning to Julia and Hermilo's home for another fiesta. It was much like the one for Our Lady of Guadalupe except that there was a charming exchange of gifts among the young people on the street. Each person received and presented a gift which was opened and displayed for all to see.

Hermilo took charge as the "conductor" of the piñatas for the children. As they broke one piñata and dove for the peanuts and candies, another would magically appear from another neighbor to be strung high above us. As the blindfolded children swung at the piñata, Hermilo would cleverly jerk the rope so the piñata would soar higher or shift positions. All the while, the others would chant hints to help locate the piñata again. The youngest children were allowed to play without blindfolds.

Eight piñatas later, the children bulging with peanuts and candy, the boom box was turned up and the dancing began. We felt right at home in the middle of the activities, probably looking quite foolish. We didn't last as long as the young people but retired about 3:00 in the morning, full of Christmas spirit and *po-zole*, a dish made by boiling a pig's head a long time and adding corn and onions. As we climbed into bed at Julia and Hermilo's house, we thanked God for this very special Christmas and dozed off with the usual night noises of La Nopalera lulling us to sleep. Soon, too soon, the morning light woke us and we looked out on the ravine crowded with houses, shacks, and litter. "Isn't it strange?" Bill observed. "I don't think I've ever seen anything more beautiful."

"And," Patty added, hugging him close, "I've never felt closer to God. God is truly present here among these people. I'm sure we've found what we've been searching for."

We had, indeed! There was no doubt that this was one of those peak experiences Maslow speaks about, or perhaps a conversion or even being born again. Thomas Merton knew that moment well when he wrote:

> At the center of my being is a point of pure nothingness which is untouched by sin or by illusion, a point of pure truth, a point or spark which belongs entirely to God....This little point of nothingness and of absolute poverty is the pure glory of God in us.[2]

We had always known the Christmas story but somehow its full impact had escaped us, perhaps because we knew very little about what it is to be poor and powerless. Here among the poor, contact with Jesus took on new meaning. Through this prism we saw all of life and ourselves in a way we had not experienced before.

More Piñatas

On the Sunday after Christmas, Sister Panchita invited us to Primero de Mayo. We were to take several piñatas since the children weren't able to have piñata parties before Christmas. The people there were so poor they couldn't afford to keep the tradition alive.

When we arrived, the colonia seemed deserted, although Sister had sent word that there would be a piñata party at 5:00 that afternoon. We slid down the embankment to Isidro's shack, where he lived with his wife and three small children. He came out shirtless and yawning while the little ones clung to the barbed wire that was strung loosely around their front door. We cringed to see the toddler biting on the barbed wire as she stared up at us.

Isidro assured Sister that he could set up the colonia's amplification system, make an announcement, and all the children would come running. That sounded simple enough but it took nearly an hour. Meanwhile, word went out among the children that we were there with piñatas and a crowd began to gather.

You have to see the poverty of the place and even smell it to begin to grasp how the people live. The children are dressed in tattered clothes, often no more than bits of underwear. They are thin and the smallest ones have swollen bellies. While the children of nearby La Nopalera are usually outgoing, these children have the look of distrust that comes from living in a newer and poorer colonia where there is no settled society.

By the time the sound system was in service atop the half-completed public building, there were over 100 children gathered around Sister Panchita as we strung up the rope for the piñatas.

Patty was given the task of selecting the children to be blindfolded, spinning them around a few times, and setting them off in the direction of the piñata with stick in hand. To our surprise, and Bill's alarm, the "stick" was an iron pole that was swung with abandon as the other children stood close by, begging for a turn. There was no arguing or competition as they did this.

When the piñata broke, all the children dove into the dust to scramble for the peanuts and candies. Another was put up and the game continued with shouting, shoving, and excitement. Many of the older children took care to see that no one was hurt in the scramble.

While the children were working on the third piñata, a herd of cattle followed by a cowboy came down the road. We newcomers were frightened and stepped down the incline to safety. The children simply made way for the cows, which are a daily part of life on their only dirt road, and then moved back to finish off the piñata.

As darkness approached, the last piñata broke and we started back to La Nopalera, this time with a trail of children running behind us waving goodbye, their dirty faces covered with smiles. Whenever we set foot in Primero de Mayo, our hearts were saddened by the awesome poverty, a poverty that dehumanizes all it touches. We wondered where hope could hide among the tar-paper shanties, the gullies carved out by last summer's rains, and the oppressive heat. And then we remembered that all hope is in Jesus, or there is none. He was there among the children and their frightened mothers, among the men without work, among the infants who were dying and the aged who might wish they could.

It must have been experiences like this one that inspired the group of Third World Christians to write:

What we discovered was that Jesus was one of us. He was born in poverty. He did not become incarnate as a king or nobleman but as one of the poor and oppressed. He took sides with the poor, supported their cause and blessed them....He even described his mission as the liberation of the downtrodden....[3]

The New Year

The afternoon of New Year's Eve we arrived at Julia and Hermilo's house to have dinner with them and their relatives. After the introductions and customary hugs, Julia asked, "Where are your bags?" We explained that we were not going to stay because they had so much company and that we would come another night. Hermilo stepped in and said, "But you can't spend New Year's Eve alone."

Bill then explained that he had left his pipe, _Mi Esposa Numero Uno_, his number one wife, at home. This had become a great transcultural joke among us but Hermilo came right back with, "Well, you must go home and get your pipe and return. There's still time before the buses stop running."

Hermilo's nephew, Antonio, a delightfully animated economics teacher from Toluca, added his sentiments. "But we are just getting acquainted. You simply must stay or we will feel you left because we're here." The twinkle in his eye told us he knew how to deal with hard-headed North Americans.

With that, everyone in the house, 13 in all, started chanting, "Go home and get your pipe, Memo." The dogs even barked as we headed back down the road to catch the bus. Bill retrieved his pipe and about two hours later we arrived back just in time to put our things on "our bed" and accompany the family to church for Mass at 8 P.M. Along the way, everyone teased Bill about his pipe and Chave asked Patty how she liked being the number two wife.

"I'm used to it," she explained. "Besides, I used to be number three behind our dog Toro. I moved up to number two when we left him in the States." With that, everyone teased Bill even more.

New Year's was celebrated almost as Christmas had been, with music, flowers, festive food, fireworks, and lots of good conversation. There we were right in the middle of it again and loving every minute. About 11:00, several of the sisters, who were making the rounds of the neighborhood celebrations, came to wish us all Happy New Year and to eat with us. How beautiful it was to see them out among the people. "More important," we reflected, "than staying in the convent praying for a good new year."

At midnight we were in the streets screaming our greetings to the New Year. It was an emotional moment as we embraced each other and our many friends. Tears of gratitude ran down our cheeks as we whispered, "Thank you, God, for bringing us here to La Nopalera. Thank you for this special year."

We had received so many invitations to visit friends in La Nopalera that we lingered most of New Year's Day. Each family welcomed us, offered us food and drink, and settled in to share stories about their lives and ours. The children gathered around, wide-eyed and innocent, trying to understand what we were saying.

At dusk, we headed back to Cuernavaca after receiving bananas from Chonita, kisses from Rico, and a large bag of mandarin oranges from Dona Juana. Our bags were bulging and our hearts were full of joy as we recalled Julia's parting words, "Don't forget. There's still Epiphany to celebrate."

The Day of the Wise

Epiphany never had deep meaning for us. We could conjure up pictures of the kings, the tyrant Herod, and the couple with the baby, but somehow the pictures hung there in our imagination like paintings in a museum, ready for an appreciation that never quite arrived. This Epiphany was different.

The church was as crowded as ever and Negro, the sisters' dog, was curled up near the baptismal font in the center aisle. After the young lectors proclaimed the readings, Sister Fidelina came to the lectern to read the gospel story of the Epiphany. Then she stepped closer to the people and asked what "Epiphany" meant. Several spoke out and sister agreed with their responses. "Yes," she said, "it's the manifestation or revelation of Jesus as the liberator and savior of the world and its poor. And the Wise Men's presence tells us that Jesus came not only to liberate the Jews but the whole world. That meant they had to share Jesus with others."

The people agreed and sister continued, "We have to share Jesus with others, too, don't we?" Once more, a loud response of agreement. "We can't be a community that cares only about itself. For example, we have among us people who have come from very far away, like the Wise Men in the gospel story, looking for Jesus." We realized Sister Fidelina was talking about us. Patty squeezed Bill's hand as sister continued. "Yes," she said, "Memo and Paty came to find Jesus among us and our task is to share him with them."

Most of the people in the chapel turned to smile at us while we sat there happy with the comparison of our search with that of the

Wise Men. Later, as we went to receive communion, people on all sides reached out to touch, hug, and kiss us as their way of saying they had opened their hearts and their community to us.

After communion, Sister Fidelina brought the life-size statue of baby Jesus over again and invited, as representatives of the community, a couple from the parish, two children, and us to hold the image as the people filed up to kiss it.

Perhaps we did understand how the Wise Men felt as they followed that star to Bethlehem and found the baby and his parents huddled together in a lean-to not unlike the ones in Primero de Mayo. Perhaps we, too, had stubbornly followed a star to where we would find Jesus. Perhaps like the Wise Men, we were searching for the One who would change the direction of the world, turning it away from injustice and sin. Perhaps, like the Wise Men, we believed in what seems to others an impossibility: the kingdom of God breaking in upon our weary, sin-sick world to show us how to make it a place of love, justice, and equality.

Like the Wise Men, we have undertaken a long and difficult journey through life armed only with faith. We believe what Jesus taught. We believe that, in spite of all the contrary evidence in the world, the kingdom of God is growing imperceptibly in our midst like a mustard seed. And as our first year in Mexico drew to a close, we believed we had, like the Wise Men, found Jesus dwelling among the poor of La Nopalera and Primero de Mayo. Unlike the Wise Men, we determined to stay with Jesus once we had found him.

A New Identity

After the celebration, we were inundated by people who had heard we were going to the States. We could see in their eyes a spark of anxiety. "You're coming back, aren't you?" they pleaded as the crowd around us grew.

"Of course we are," Bill explained. "This is our home now. We're going to visit our family, but we'll return in three weeks." Some of the children exclaimed, "Three weeks?" as if that were forever. In the end, we convinced everyone that we were not going to stay away.

The next day at our literacy class we explained again that we would be back in class in three weeks.When our friends expressed their disappointment, we assured them that we'd return. These people have had so much experience with loved ones leaving for the United States or even other parts of Mexico never to be heard from again.

Sister Tonya, the youngest of the sisters, was watching the commotion, waiting to invite us to the convent to wish us a safe and pleasant trip. When we got there, we were seated in the room that serves as the sisters' living area, parish office, and dining room. All six sisters were grinning as if they had something funny to share with us. "Memo," Sister Tonya asked, "remember when the children began calling her Madre Paty, Mother Paty, because they call all of the sisters Madre? Then you observed that not only the children but many of the adults called her that. 'That's Madre Paty, the *Madre con esposo*, the Mother with a husband.'"

Sister Tonya paused as we all laughed. "Well, we wanted to tell you and Paty before you go to the United States that the people have begun to call you 'Madre Memo.'" We all laughed and repeated, "Madre Memo, Madre Memo." Bill grinned from ear to ear.

The sisters were obviously pleased that in the people's search to identify our role in the community, they had finally settled on the idea that we were somehow related with the sisters. They knew Memo couldn't be Padre Memo, for that was what they call the priests, but he was there loving the people as the sisters did and so he must be something like a madre. The name stuck. Ever after the sisters and many of the people introduce Memo as Madre Memo.

Questions to Answer

As this month of celebrations came to an end, we had grasped another aspect of that elusive spirit of the poor. There were, however, two questions we had not yet answered: What were the people celebrating? Why were they so able to enter into such a carefree spirit of celebration when their lives were ravaged by poverty and oppression?

It was evident that there were no clear boundaries between their daily life and religion. Everything they did was religious; every event in the church was a part of daily life. They had allowed Jesus to become incarnate in their lives. There was no special language for the church, no separation of church and state, no rituals that had lost their meaning. Life was of a single piece and Jesus was as much a part of it as they themselves were.

For the first time, we understood that the incarnation, if it was to be successful, required more than an action by God. It demanded that people welcome Jesus into their lives. Mary did, and Joseph and the shepherds and the Wise Men, too. In La Nopalera, simple people were still welcoming Jesus, taking his presence as a reality in their day-to-day lives. They did not go to church to find Jesus for he was everywhere among them. It was this unselfconscious realization of his presence that endowed them with dignity. In spite of poverty and oppression, they were his people and he was their God. It was as simple as that. Their celebrations were an opportunity to reaffirm what was an integral part of their lives.

To us, the incarnation had always seemed an important but somehow churchy reality. It was an abstraction we were taught to believe but not to experience or feel. We celebrated it in an official way on Christmas but even that celebration was sandwiched between other rituals: gift-giving, Santa Claus, family togetherness. The incarnation belonged in church and reflected not what was happening now but what had happened centuries ago. For us, Christmas had never been what it was in La Nopalera, because religion had been allowed to claim Christianity as its own special interest, the province of priests, ministers, and those who called themselves "religious people."

The people of La Nopalera understood that they were with God and God was with them. Whether they went to church or not did not alter this fact. God was first and foremost in the community, the men and women who shared their daily lives. Church and liturgy were important only as means to intensify that awareness and celebrate that presence. So, too, were the ancient rituals some of them anchored in their pre-Christian past. No matter where the celebrations originated, they now spoke of one reality, the presence of Jesus and his mother, Mary, in their daily lives.

They had entered into that peace that surpasses all understanding, the peace that was and is the center of the Christmas mystery. It was of this peace that the Latin American Bishops wrote in their landmark conference at Medellin in 1968:

> Peace is the fruit of love. It is the expression of true fellowship among human beings, a union given by Christ, prince of peace, in reconciling all persons with the Father. Human solidarity cannot truly take effect, unless it is done in Christ who gives peace that the world cannot give. Love is the soul of justice. Christians who work for social justice should always cultivate peace and love in their hearts.
>
> Peace with God is the basic foundation of internal and social peace. Therefore, where this social peace does not exist, there will we find social, political, economic and cultural inequalities, there will we find the rejection of the peace of the Lord, and a rejection of the Lord himself.[4]

We also wondered why these people celebrated with such ease, with such naturalness? The answer was as obvious as it was so often overlooked: They did not take themselves as individuals very seriously; they had achieved what the gospel calls becoming like little children. This was possible because their community life, not their individual lives, was the focus of their thought. For them, the teaching of Jesus had never been reduced to a set of rules that individuals must obey to be saved. Rather, his message was good news to the community, that they were and are the children of God. The individual struggle is always to give more fully to the community, always to care more about others and less about one-self. Few even thought about their own salvation, their own slate of rights and wrongs, their own worthiness before God.

This did not mean that individuals were free to do as they pleased, to rape, plunder, and participate in every form of evil. In fact, the concern for community was so intense that it prohibited them from many forms of selfishness that we in the First World rarely think of as sin: competition, over-consumption, individual ownership in the face of community need. Those who sinned, sinned against the community and the community punished them with its own subtle forms of excommunication. Thus, if you were at ease with the community, you could be at ease with God and could celebrate as unselfconsciously as a child.

Carlos Mesters, one of the early lights of liberation theology, understood this well:

> In a sense we can say that the tabernacle of the church is to be found where the people come together around the word of God. That could be called the church's holy of holies. Remember that no one was allowed to enter the holy of holies, except the high priest, and he was allowed in only once a year. In this holy of holies no one is master—except God and the people. It is there that the Holy Spirit is at work; and where the Spirit is at work there is freedom.The deepest and ultimate roots of the freedom sought by all are to be found there, in these small groups where the people meet around the word of God.[5]

The sisters, who represented the official church in La Nopalera, seemed to understand this at the deepest level. They never insist-ed that people attend church services nor did they show favorit-ism to those who did. They spoke constantly of the community and rarely of individual, isolated morality. They saw themselves as helpers of the community; their first loyalty was to the people and not to an institution, many of whose leaders lived a lifestyle that prohibited them from membership in this community. God was with the people in this newly discovered holy of holies and so were they. For them, and for us, that was enough.

It was these two characteristics of the people of La Nopalera that we had experienced as they accepted us into their lives: a spirit of welcome and an unselfconscious love of the community. These characteristics were at the base of all community and cele-bration, and so of all good liturgy as well.

Those who had the spirit of the poor knew the meaning of Christmas, of incarnation, of welcoming strangers. They knew how to celebrate them with gusto and abandon.

Chapter Ten

A Time of Suffering

We share in the suffering of many of our friends as they cope with the violence poverty brings. These experiences reveal a new and deeper revelation of the meaning of Lent, Holy Week, and Easter.

It is not easy to live in Mexico with its corrupt and repressive government, erratic and contaminated water supply, ever-present stench of raw sewage, diarrhea, dysentery, typhoid, endless lines, and general chaos. There is epidemic malnutrition. In Cuernavaca, drinking water is contaminated with chemicals and bacteria and yet the city boasts of having more swimming pools per capita than any other city in the world. While many of our poor friends haul water in buckets up and down steep ravines or pay to have water delivered from a filthy water truck, the rich sun themselves by their crystal-clear pools. While poor men, women, and children are climbing in and out of dumpsters in wealthy neighborhoods scavenging for rapidly rotting food and even cardboard, the rich dine in fine restaurants. This is the reality we have seen in Mexico.

We wondered whether it was unique to our area or was a part of the larger picture of the Third World. We had traveled to other Third World countries, but had never shared the lives of the poor. We have read the theology and sociology of the poor, but these were a step removed from personal experience, an experience we could trust.

In late January the answer to our questions arrived, bright, beautiful and full of life in the person of our daughter Angel, a Maryknoll lay missioner from Brazil. She was on a two-week vacation after living and working among the Brazilian poor for two years. She opened to us a wider vision of Third World life, its grinding poverty and unbelievable injustice.

Angel was immediately comfortable with our friends in La Nopalera and they with her, even though she spoke Portuguese and not Spanish. They showered her with attention, gifts, and welcoming love. Angel talked about her friends in Brazil at one of the Sunday celebrations and her description of their lives might well have been of life in La Nopalera.

The Daily Violence of Poverty
One evening, as we left La Nopalera, Angel remarked, "I can't believe we are walking around this neighborhood at night. We could never do this in São Miguel Paulista. I'm beginning to realize how violent poverty is in Brazil. Why, in our area, the leading cause of death between the ages of 5 and 50 is homicide." We both took a deep breath; such a statistic is enough to strike terror into the parents of a 26-year-old woman living so far away.

We talked long into the night about violence. We had seen isolated acts, such as the young man who was stoned to death next to the church, or the man who was strangled in a local barber shop. Nature could be violent, too: the heavy rain that destroyed a hillside house with everyone living in it. Yet, violence was not a way of life in La Nopalera. Our situation seemed very different from São Paulo and we were glad.

Angel talked about the frustration in Brazil brought on by politicians' promises that life would be better, but it actually got worse. Our Mexican friends, on the other hand, did not expect life to get better. It had always been harsh and they expected nothing else. Perhaps this was the reason for the difference in the levels of violence among the poor of Brazil and Mexico.

All too quickly we were standing in the Mexico City airport saying goodbye and crying in spite of our efforts to appear calm. Angel had to return to the poor of her community. We had to remain faithful to ours. On the way home we reminisced about Angel's life and how our almost-always-frightened-of-anything-new little girl had grown into a faith-filled, determined, fearless, and compassionate young woman. Only God could work such a miracle.

Angel's visit had warmed our hearts and stimulated our minds. It confirmed our fear that Mexico's poverty and injustice were only a part of a pattern that included many lands. While we were pondering her comments about the lack of violence in La Nopalera and Primero de Mayo, things suddenly changed. Murder and violence appeared on a scale we could hardly believe. The whole of Lent was spent burying the dead and comforting the afflicted.

A New Violence

We were aware that life itself was violent in La Nopalera and Primero de Mayo. The structures our friends lived in bred violence of every sort. We knew in our hearts that what the Christians for Socialism had said in the final document of their convention in 1972 about violence was true, however much we disagreed with other parts of their document.

> The economic and social structures of Latin American countries are grounded on oppression and injustice, which in turn is a result of our capitalist dependence on the great power centers. In each nation small minorities serve the cause of international capitalism and its accomplices. Using

every means in their power, they seek to maintain a situation that was created to benefit themselves. This structural injustice is, in fact, violence, whether it is open or disguised. Those who have exploited the weak for centuries and who wish to keep doing this use de facto violence against them. This violence is often veiled under the guise of a fallacious order and legality, but it is violence and injustice nonetheless. It is not human, and hence it is not Christian.[1]

This was the global picture played out locally in a lack of water, electricity, jobs, and medical care. But so far, the violence we had seen was confined to institutions. We had not experienced personal violence, which we might have expected would follow the structural violence all around us.

Suddenly everything changed. It all began with our friend Maria de la Paz, who was a grandmother in her fifties and a vibrant part of our literacy class and a member of one of our base Christian communities. There were a dozen people in this community, and in six weeks, three of the families were shattered by violence. Three people were dead and another three had to be hospitalized. A cloud of depression and fear descended on the most vulnerable of our friends.

As Lent began, Maria de la Paz was attending a Sunday afternoon neighborhood celebration of a girl's fifteenth birthday, an important celebration in Mexico. The celebration took place next to the family's shack perched on a cliff overlooking the small stream that flowed below Primero de Mayo. The houses are close together; there are no streets, only rough, very steep paths down to the stream. What happens in one yard affects the lives of everyone nearby. Two older teenage boys began to quarrel in an adjoining yard. They had probably been drinking and became more and more abusive of each other.

Maria yelled at the boys, asking that they stop the arguing which was ruining the birthday party. The boys became quiet but were angry at the reprimand. They walked home, got a gun, and calmly shot Maria and a seven-year-old girl, and killed a mother of six children, all of whom were at the party. The others sat stunned. The killers and their family simply packed up their belongings and left the colonia while the police did nothing. There was no government aid for the father left with six children, or for the seriously wounded Maria de la Paz and the girl. Neighbors carried Maria and the girl up the steep ravine to the road at the top of the settlement. Others ran to La Nopalera, a half-mile away, to find a taxi to take them to the hospital.

The next day, as soon as we heard about the slaughter, we rushed to the hospital only to be told that visitors' hours were over. While we negotiated with the head nurse, a man of about forty sat opposite us in the open foyer. He was covered with blood which ran from his body into a pool on the tile floor. People stepped gingerly to avoid the growing puddle. The hospital staff did not seem to notice his pain or the anguish of his young wife. After negotiating for a half-hour, we were allowed into a ward where we found Maria with twenty other men and women. She had been operated on to remove the bullet from her back, but the doctor could not remove it and sewed her up, bullet and all. When we found her she was colorless and in great pain. All around her, the sick were moaning and thrashing about in their beds.

Maria began to cry, not for herself but for her teenage daughter who sat next to her bed and for her granddaughter Anna, who was still in the colonia. Between sobs, she told us that Griselda had not eaten all day and that she did not know where Anna was. She had no money to feed her daughter or to pay the hospital bill and no way of finding out what had happened to Anna. Not only was she sick and badly wounded, she was helpless and poor.

We gave Maria what money we had to feed Griselda and were able to discover that family members had taken Anna in. By the end of the week, the poor in Primero de Mayo had taken up a collection to pay for her hospital expenses. Months later, Maria was barely able to walk.

Soon another incident involved our Primero de Mayo community friends Soltera and Jesus and Soltera's brother Carmerino and his wife, Ester, all of whom were among the poorest people we had met. One Saturday, Carmerino had an argument with a man whose house he was building. The man hacked him to death with a machete. Carmerino was not yet thirty, the father of four children, one an infant who had not yet even been named. His murder was so savage that even the family could not recognize him.

The dead man's family fled to their ancestral home in Guerrero to bury Carmerino and to decide whether or not to return to the growing violence of Primero de Mayo. Soltera and Jesus returned first and later Ester, the dead man's widow. There was no work and very little water in their native village and so life in Primero de Mayo with all its violence was better than life in the campo where people were starving to death.

In this case, as in the shooting of Maria de la Paz, the police did nothing.

And then violence struck our special friends, Julia and Hermilo, vital members of the church in La Nopalera. Three drunk teenagers seized their daughter Mago and her boyfriend Goyo on their way home from the church at 7:00 one evening. They beat them both and then one of the boys abducted Mago, a 22-year-old engineering student.

At 6:00 the next morning, Julia and her niece Chave appeared at our door. "They have taken Mago," they sobbed. "We have been searching all night. Can we use your telephone, please?" There are no telephones in La Nopalera.

Trying to control our panic, we dressed quickly and joined the search. Together we rushed across town on the Ruta to the state police, since the local police had refused to do anything. At the barracks, we were shunted from one official to another for over an hour and a half. Finally we were told that the official who had to sign the papers opening an investigation would not be in his office until early that afternoon. Until he signed the papers, the police could not begin an investigation.

"By that time my daughter may be dead," Julia sobbed as the clerk turned his face and looked impassively out the window. We waited for the official who finally came and signed the form. He told us that in a few days a policeman would call to begin the investigation. We wept.

Meanwhile Hermilo had to beg to be allowed to take the day off to join in the search. His employer reluctantly agreed, but warned him that more than one day would be cause for termination. Frantically, he joined the search and the police demanded money to initiate the investigation.

That afternoon one of the kidnapper's aunt and uncle appeared at Hermilo's house with Mago badly beaten and barely able to stand. As far as we could tell, she was not raped, probably because she bled so badly from the beating that the young drunks became frightened. One of them had taken her to a relative's house in Cuernavaca, where she continued to bleed. In the morning a doctor stopped the bleeding with a bandage. As it turned out, Mago's nose was broken in four places and required surgery.

The police came two days later and demanded more money before they would arrest the wrong-doers. This was paid, but two of the young offenders were back on the street in a few days. The third has never been located and is reported to have fled to the United States.

About this time, Mauro, another member of our base community at Primero de Mayo, was shot to death early one Sunday evening. Since then, there have been at least six other killings in the area, including an outbreak of gang warfare that left two dead of icepick wounds and seven others hospitalized. Most of the violence was to innocent people, brought on by alcohol and drugs, which in turn are an escape from the oppression of the economic situation. What Angel told us about Brazil was beginning to happen in La Nopalera.

Gustavo Gutierrez has seen this reality and delved into its causes.

The true face of Latin America is emerging in all its naked

ugliness. It is not simply or primarily a question of low educational standards, a limited economy, an unsatisfactory legal system, or inadequate legal institutions. What we are faced with is a situation that takes no account of the dignity of human beings, or their most elemental needs, that does not provide for their biological survival, or their basic right to be free and autonomous. Poverty, injustice, alienation and the exploitation of human beings by other human beings combine to form a situation that the Medellin conference did not hesitate to call institutional violence.[2]

We were seeing the true face of Latin America in all its naked ugliness. Friends were dead, others maimed for life. Physicians and hospitals offered almost no care to those who could not afford to pay for it. The police demanded bribes before opening an investigation and took no interest in preventing further violence. Television programs and home videos, many imported from the U.S., encouraged gang warfare, drugs, and violence, especially violence against women. We stood at the side of our poor friends and with them we suffered their pain. This was Lent in La Nopalera and Primero de Mayo. Daily we encountered Christ suffering in his people.

The Violence of the Sects

A parish priority this year, as last, was visiting the homes of all the Catholics in the area to invite them to the lenten talks held on three evenings the week before Holy Week. The base communities organized and carried out this task, with the admonition that members not bother families that belong to Protestant sects in order to show respect for their religious beliefs.

These sects in La Nopalera, and indeed throughout Mexico, Central, and South America, are usually small, fundamentalist groups with evangelical roots in the United States. They bear almost no similarity to the mainline Protestant denominations, but rather resemble extreme American fundamentalist churches. A criterion for membership is renunciation of their Catholic traditions and pieties and a militant stance against all things Catholic, including the great celebrations like Christmas. This, of course, leads to conflicts within families and among neighbors. Children of sect members are taught to avoid contact with the heathen Catholics. It is sad to see them marching resolutely down the street, Bible in hand, eyes downcast, on their way to the humble churches that dot the landscape.

The sect leaders come from among the poor people and usually do not have much education or training. In our area, one of the sect leaders rules his family and flock with an iron fist. The theology that emerges from his sect and ones like it promotes docility and personal conversion. It strongly denounces involvement in politics, thus making its members malleable to the will of the repressive government.

The sect members are regarded as traitors to their tradition, and because they do not usually mix with the others in the area to help with community projects like street construction, they are resented. On the positive side, the pressure of families and friends joining the sects has caused Catholics to focus more attention on community-building, Bible study, and reflection. The more astute among the Catholics have analyzed, with the help of the sisters, what draws people to the sects; they have tried to respond to their needs within the Catholic community. Still, there remains deep resentment for the social chaos the sects have caused.

Like poverty itself, the sects are a violence wreaked against the poor. They destroy family ties, break ancient traditions, promise salvation in exchange for passivity, and create confusion among the most vulnerable members of the community. Most of these groups begin as outreaches of independent fundamentalist churches in the States. Some claim that the U.S. government and business interests favor them and support some of their activities. Whether that is so or not, these groups play into the hands of the Mexican government's repressive policies by stilling voices that would otherwise be raised in dissent.

What is most ironic about this form of religious oppression is that its ultimate cause may be the upper hierarchy of the Catholic church. Penny Lernoux, America's leading expert on the church in Latin America, wrote shortly before her death:

> Ironically, the Vatican's refusal to countenance a more pluralistic, lay-oriented church has contributed to the growth of U.S.-sponsored Protestant fundamentalist churches in Latin America. As Archbishop Camara observed, Rome is unable to comprehend "the good that is done in the name of liberation theology," particularly the base communities. Yet, the communities are the best hope to counter the spread of generally anti-Catholic, born-again churches....Surveys by Catholic institutions showed that wherever base communities flourished, fundamentalist churches were unlikely to gain recruits.[3]

Palm Sunday

Lent at La Nopalera, and at the other four chapels the sisters pastor in the area, was orchestrated with a combination of themes, symbols, liturgies, and discussions, all of which built to a crescendo for Holy Week and Easter. Everywhere the theme of violence and oppression was dominant. Week by week the crowds grew in size as people were swept up in the approaching celebration of Jesus' passion, death, and resurrection.

When we arrived at the designated gathering place for the Palm Sunday procession in the heat and dust of late afternoon, the various lenten committees had coordinated their work well. Since the date coincided with the eleventh anniversary of the assassination of Archbishop Oscar Romero of San Salvador, a large group of children waved high above the crowd enlarged photographs of him and other Latin American martyrs. Members of base communities carried posters with biblical quotes and protests against injustice as they followed the procession up the steep hill to the church.

We joined the throng in singing and waving palms woven by local artisans into the shape of Jesus on the cross. How much like the original triumphal march of Jesus into Jerusalem was this ragtag procession that included, besides the people, roosters, dogs, and donkeys. No one would have been surprised to look up and see Jesus mounted on one of the donkeys, so moving was the scene. We filled the church and overflowed into the yard as the celebration began. Feet shifted and children strained to see above the crowd as the lectors read the passion narrative with emotion. As we looked around at the impassive Native Americans, we sensed their complete concentration and identification with the suffering of Jesus.

After the passion narrative, Sister Fidelina asked the people to break into groups and discuss two questions: "Who killed Jesus?" and "Why did they kill him?" The people in our group quickly identified the religious leaders and the high priests of the Jews as the perpetrators; they were the rich and powerful, they reasoned, who feared that the poor people who listened to what Jesus was preaching would turn against them and demand justice.

Soon Sister Fidelina asked representatives from different groups to report on their discussion. Weaving these ideas into a powerful reflection on the meaning of Jesus' passion, she reminded the people that most of those who marched into Jerusalem with Jesus soon betrayed him. Several people offered short reflections on why people today betray others when things get tough. Sister drew the homily to a close by tying in the assassination of Oscar Romero and the countless other Latin American martyrs who offered up their lives as Jesus did in the cause of justice and love.

Thus Holy Week began with a religious insight that was new to us. And we reminded each other of the words of Archbishop Oscar Romero whose assassination we remembered that day.

Our pascal hope gives meaning to the outcast, to the illiterate, to those dying of malnutrition. It not only shouts that

things should not be like this but says to the one suffering
"You will perhaps die like this. Offer it in redemption." That
is why I have said...that all those who have offered up their
lives, their heroism, their sacrifice—if they have really offered it with a sincere desire to give true liberty and dignity
to our people—that they are incorporating themselves into
the great sacrifice of Christ.[4]

Holy Thursday

People do not work on Holy Thursday or Good Friday unless it is
absolutely necessary. They have a long tradition of celebrating the
Last Supper with elaborate symbols and liturgy. In La Nopalera,
for example, they came in large numbers to the liturgy in which a
priest from a neighboring parish washed the feet of representatives of the various parish groups. He then reflected on the meaning of Jesus' actions that night for us today as well as for his first
disciples.

Good Friday

Finally, after almost forty days of intense and consistent preparation, we reached that ignominious day on which Jesus carried his
cross, was crucified, died, and was buried. When we arrived at
the church at 9:00 A.M., we found a few people in the church patiently waiting near the huge, heavy, wooden cross standing on
end behind the unadorned altar. Sr. Fidelina explained that we
would end our journey by joining the group from Los Pinos chapel at the last station. Then she led us in a reflection on the first station and invited representatives from various groups in the parish
to carry the cross to the second station. Sister Panchita recited a
list of crosses the poor people of La Nopalera carry as the cross
was lifted and ceremoniously carried down the road to the second
station, followed by an expanding crowd.

After the prayer and reflection at the second station, Sister Panchita invited the children to carry the cross and recited a litany of
crosses our poor children carry each day of their lives: malnutrition and the sicknesses it brings, violence, inadequate clothing

and housing, death of parents, brothers, and sisters, having to go to work before completing school, the absence of parents in the home because of flight to the States to find work.

As our little friends lifted the cross, tears flowed down our faces, tears of compassion and of indignation at the injustices these children must suffer, so innocent, so like Jesus on the cross. In the three hours of our procession that wound through the back streets gathering people with flowers along the way, different groups were invited to carry the cross and a litany of abuses they suffered were proclaimed. When they called for the viejitos (old people), Patty decided it was time to carry the cross with them. When we reached the bottom of the hill to meet the people from Los Pinos at the final station, we had become a huge, exhausted crowd, and out of nowhere appeared cold fruit juice for everyone.

Holy Saturday

Holy Saturday afternoon was quiet as we arrived in Primero de Mayo for our base community meeting. There was an atmosphere of mourning as a few people emerged from their homes to join us in our observation of Jesus' burial. As we did this, we could feel the darkness and stench of the sealed tomb as we read together the passage describing it. Seeing our friends perched there along the sides of the ravine, sitting on packing crates and rocks, it seemed that they were closed up in the tomb with Jesus, awaiting his resurrection and theirs. How hopeless their lives appeared, crushed by poverty and oppression, abandoned and rejected by the world. Yet they clung to life and dared to believe that their own suffering will lead to resurrection with Jesus.

In spite of the indignities they endure, they are struggling to break out of the tomb and live as true sons and daughters of God. For them, Holy Week and Easter are today lived out in the stench and violence of poverty. Most of all, Jesus' story is their story. He is no story-book character, but flesh of their flesh, bone of their bone. He is as real as they are. He has suffered what they are suffering. He stands by their side, holds their hand, and teaches them how to bring the kingdom of God into the world. He promises resurrection to those who believe and live as he did. These simple, illiterate people take Jesus at his word. Theirs is an innocent and child-like trust that other Christians might well envy and learn from.

As the sun set behind the distant mountains, we reflected on the resurrection and closed with prayer. Most of us slowly made our way back from the ravine after filling pails of water to haul to the church for the priest to bless during the outdoor Easter Vigil Mass.

People came from every direction with babies in arms and toddlers struggling to keep up. We greeted each other in our usual manner while the sisters concluded their preparations. The church yard rapidly overflowed as Padre Cristobal lit the Easter fire and passed the light of Christ in the form of lighted candles that people clutched in their hands. A soft, warm glow filled the night as we settled in for the Easter liturgy.

Easter Day

The next afternoon, Easter, we caught sight of a crudely drawn poster in the church. Dominating the poster was a human figure who had broken the chains that bound him. Around the figure were the faces of other, obviously poor, people. Lettered carefully on the poster were these words:

The Mass was born during
a fiesta of liberation
of the people of Israel.

Today the Mass remains
a fiesta of liberation
for it remembers and presents again
the resurrection of Jesus.

This resurrection guarantees
the *liberation* of a people

who are united together
to respect human rights,
to demand just and humane living conditions,
and equality and fairness for all.

This was the resurrection theme we celebrated in La Nopalera. It harkened to our distant Jewish past, focused on the reality of Jesus' resurrection, and in a few words translated that past into a dynamic, living present. Sacred and secular were united; religion and politics were one. The resurrection of Jesus was no shadowy event lost in theological controversy, but a promise and a challenge for the people in La Nopalera today.

The idea for the poster, we later learned, came from a quote in a book by Brazilian theologian Leonardo Boff, but the drawing was the idea of a parish teenager. Some teens were trying to make sense of the resurrection when one of the sisters had given them the Boff quote. They turned it over in their own minds and decided to share it with the entire parish by means of the poster because it meant so much to them.

In the climate of violence that had struck the community that Lent, the words had special meaning: human rights, just living conditions, fairness for all. Violence opposed all of these.

We began to understand that the poor spend much of their lives coping with violence, the violence done by alcohol-deadened individuals, the violence of frustrated family members, the systematic violence of the rich and powerful, and even the violence of nature itself. Jesus encouraged those with the spirit of the poor to struggle against this violence, even heroically at times. Yet their struggle does not appear to overcome their own sense of composure or patience. They are sure that God is on their side and will in time help them overcome their oppression. Perhaps this is the hope, present even in the youngest, that keeps them from desperation and discouragement.

Easter, we concluded, was the special feast of the poor. They were like Jesus in the tomb, awaiting their resurrection. Since he had risen, they were quite sure that they, too, will one day over-come their oppression. This hope anchored so many other charac-teristics of those with the spirit of the poor. Archbishop Romero put it this way:

And you will see, my beloved poor...oppressed...outcasts... sick, that the dawn of the resurrection is now beginning to shine. The hour is coming for our people. And we should wait for it, as Christians, not only in its particular political dimensions, but in its dimensions of faith and hope.[5]

—Chapter Eleven—

Bringing It Together

*After walking with the Mexican poor and loving them,
we begin to understand what it means to have the spirit
of the poor.*

We have spent two years on our Mexican journey but we have
just begun our search. We can with caution and care speak Spanish. We understand something of the rhythm of the lives of the
poor, the important days, the effects of constant poverty, the suffering, the joy in simple things, and the awareness of community
that pervades everything they do and everything they are. But
this is only a beginning.

Sacred and Secular

In trying to understand the spirit of the poor, our thoughts keep
returning to the insights of that unusual religious anthropologist
Mircea Eliade and his descriptions of secular persons and their
opposites. It is difficult to describe the opposite of Eliade's secular
person. He or she is a person who lives and breathes the sacred, so

much so that life without God is unimaginable. We will call such a person "religious," knowing that this may cause some confusion. This distinction between the religious and secular person is something much deeper than membership in a church, adherence to its rules or even to its leadership. It is, according to Eliade, a cultural phenomenon, a reality that a society confers on its members. Not all religious people are good nor are all secular people evil. This crucial difference between the secular and the religious person is not a matter of morality, piety, dogma, or zeal for a cause. It is deeper than that.

The Christian version of the religious person is convinced that the world is in the hands of God and is good because God is good. The religious person knows that there is nothing that can outwit God or quietly assume divine power. God is in charge. This is God's world, which is governed by an eternal plan of an eternal creator. To be human is to respect, honor, and listen to the world, and to God's plan for it, as far as that can be known. It is not our place to conquer it or turn it to goals entirely our own, however good. Whatever efforts the religious person makes to effect change are puny. The religious person does make them, however, but at God's bidding and is not disappointed when they do not appear to come to a good end, for God has purposes that humans may not understand.

By contrast, a secular person—and most of us who live in the industrialized countries of the world are secular persons—may repeat the prayers and formulas or perform the acts of piety an ancient tradition left us. Yet, to be secularized does not mean what it once meant. For example, consider the modern Catholic or Protestant who holds on to the prayers and pieties of childhood. She says her prayers every morning and night, goes to parish meetings twice a week, and never misses church on Sunday. Yet, these times of prayer are compartments in her life—a few minutes or a few hours here or there. Her awareness of the sacred is, by and large, limited only to these moments because her daily life crowds out an abiding, unselfconscious awareness of God.

Being less aware of the sacred is only one part of being secular. The religious person spontaneously manifests a complete dependence on God, but the secular person is constantly troubled by the interaction of the natural and supernatural and the point where one begins and the other ends. Such a person may believe in divine providence but is never quite sure how to act out that belief. The devout woman, for example, whose child is ill will pray, but she will also seek the best medical care. When the child is well again, she will repeat traditional words of thanksgiving to God, but will also tell her neighbors how wonderful the doctor was who "saved" her child. The religious person might also go to the doctor, but for her it would be only God who spared her child.

The secular person sees all around him problems to be solved: illness, homelessness, war, reform of institutions, to name but a few. He feels a responsibility to search for and use the means necessary to "solve these problems." Because he feels responsible, he is often discouraged, troubled, and even depressed. His culture insists that every "problem" has a solution and being resolute means continuing the struggle to find it. Thus, we glorify the scientist who spends countless lonely hours in the laboratory seeking the cause of a disease and call him successful when he finds it or a failure when he does not.

We are born into a culture, a set of circumstances and assumptions. Unless we make unusual efforts we rarely if ever escape these assumptions and beliefs. We can be morally good as a religious person or a secular person. Yet, being morally good is not what Christianity is about. Jesus, after all, spent a good bit of his time with those who were not morally good. What he asked of his followers was not so much morality as faith, a reliance on God, an awareness of the sacred. He stated again and again that it was the poor and powerless who had that insight and the rich who did not.

This is the mystery of Christianity, the stillpoint at the center of its soul, around which all dogma, liturgy, prayer, and morality revolve. This is why Jesus, who loved the rich young man who kept all the commandments, told him to sell what he had, give it to the poor, and then follow him. The implication was obvious to the church which remembered the story and treasured it enough to enshrine it in the gospels. One cannot follow Jesus without the total dependence on God that poverty brings. Another of his sayings: You cannot serve God and Mammon. And, of course, that mighty first beatitude: Happy are those who have the spirit of the poor; theirs is the kingdom of heaven. It is the poor who have not been corrupted by a desire for wealth who are naturally religious. The rest of us can only hope to learn from them and treasure their wisdom.

In our Mexican sojourn, we have discovered something of this wisdom and begun to embrace the spirit of the poor, the goal of our life in Cuernavaca. Like all great changes in life, however, we have thus far done so only to a degree; there is much more here for us to grasp and do. Each day brings new understanding and insight into the meaning of life itself. Each day brings new friends, new stories, new ideals, new reasons to hope that the world will change and the kingdom of God will one day come.

We must try to become religious people who live in the realm of the sacred. This means no more and no less than standing in the sandals of the poor, accepting life as they do, and challenging injustice in all its forms. It means seeing God everywhere, in good things and in bad, in sickness and in health, in joy and in sadness, in every word that comes from the world God rules.

Childhood Images

In addition to this fundamental insight into the spirit of the poor, others shook our old stereotypes. Raised in Catholic church before Vatican II, we came to Mexico with many assumptions and ideals born unconsciously in that era, thoughts still clinging to our souls even after years of work in church renewal. All the books on liberation theology, the history of Mexico and Latin America, and the sociology and economics of the Third World had not fully prepared us for what we discovered. Nor had our short visits to poor countries for, although they had alerted us to the enormity of world poverty, they had not exposed us to the depth of that reality and its effects on the lives of the people who lived with it. Our assumptions and ideals were subtle, the kind of taken-for-granted pillars of our thinking that we had never deliberately put into words and examined thoughtfully. They lived as vague images in our unconscious.

Passivity

Two of these unconscious images so popular in North American thought were dashed for us forever during this time. The first was formed in us, we are sure, while we were still children. During those countless Saturday afternoons in our neighborhood movie theaters, we had watched cowardly, ingratiating Mexicans flee before our Anglo heroes. Mexican men wore outlandish hats and dozed comfortably under a convenient tree or on a hacienda porch, escaping the noonday sun. Mexican women were subservient creatures surrounded by a tribe of ragged little children. They lit countless candles and found solace in obscure devotions that always seemed to focus on some strange devotion to the Virgin Mary. Mexicans were unambitious happy little brown people content with their lot in life because they knew no other. We North Americans were, of course, superior in every way.

This myth of the happy Mexican waiting to be conquered by the dashing Anglo hero had infected our thinking, no matter how much we would have denied it had we understood it was at work in us. More recently, that image had been translated into catch terms such as Third World, underdeveloped countries, overpopulated areas, pre-industrial nations, and even Chicano. Our newer images were the "Frito Bandito," pictures of illegal aliens crossing the Rio Grande, and indolent Latin Americans munching corn chips. This myth corresponds with the "victim ego state" Carl Jung described. The person in his or her victim mode enjoys suffering, seeks defeat, revels in persecution, and lives in a state of mild depression relieved by times of raucous celebration.

The media taught us the solution to the problems of Mexico's poor: They must work harder and have fewer children. The great stumbling block to their becoming more like us, the media said, was the hierarchy of the Catholic church, which forbade birth control and failed to encourage hard work and competition as did churches in the States.

Without realizing it, we had linked this media-myth about the Mexican poor to a religious ideal we had learned as children. When we did this, we changed the meaning of the facts. What the media claimed were negative personality traits—passivity, for example—we had made positive. Yet, we had never investigated the facts the media gave us. We assumed they were true, but because of our training we gave these "facts" a new meaning, what politicians would call "controlling the spin" (or meaning) of events.

Like so many Catholics of our generation, we had come to imagine that Jesus called his disciples out of the world to a life of prayer and contemplation. Our religious pictures depicted Jesus with a passively sweet smile. Our prayers exalted victimhood. Our religious heroes were those who suffered without complaint at the hands of the violent. Passivity was the ideal of the devout Catholic in the United States from the 1940s to the early 1960s. It remains so for many Catholics and for most evangelical and fundamentalist sects even today.

When the Mexican poor appeared passive, as they did so often in our movies, we assumed that this imagined passivity must be a kind of holiness. It was a holiness we admired but, of course, rarely imitated. Without realizing it, we had two very different sets of heroes. As Catholics, we admired the passivity we thought we saw in poor Mexicans. As Americans, however, our heroes continued to be the Anglo cowboys who went forth to crusade for justice. Because the secular and the sacred were neatly divided in American life, we never noticed this inconsistency in our thought. We wanted to be like the aggressive cowboys while admiring the passive Mexicans. This satisfied our ideals as Catholics and as Americans, no matter how contradictory these two ideals were.

Images like these lying deep within our unconscious made it easy to idealize the poor, especially the passive poor. Unless we were careful, we realized, the poor could easily become objects of our charity. We would love them as they appeared to be, not as they really were; we would believe that our part in a relationship with them was to share what we had. That charity would have absolved us of any responsibility of going deeper into a relationship, of creating a situation in which we were truly equals with the poor, a situation in which we would receive as well as give.

Over and over again, we found these old images invading our thoughts. To be powerless and poor, the old images said, was to be automatically good. Yet, our experience denied this. Some of the poor were as greedy as any American we had ever met. They trampled on the rights of their fellow poor and exalted in the tiny bits of power and affluence that came their way. Some were violent. Some were alcoholics and abusers of drugs. Some husbands beat their wives; some wives cheated on their husbands. One could write a soap opera situated in La Nopalera or Primero de Mayo as easily as in Dallas. Yet, with all this said, there was a difference between the poor and the rich when they tried to follow the gospel and welcome Jesus into their lives. There was a reality to the words, "the spirit of the poor," and we have begun to discover, admire, and desire to embrace it.

Heedless Heroes

The second image, equally romantic, was that of the crusading hero who had gone off to the mountains to fight the unjust establishment. This image was formed in us by reading about the heroes of this generation, men like Che Guevara, Camillo Torres, and the Sandinista revolutionaries. Cuernavaca itself claimed three such local heroes: Emiliano Zapata of revolutionary fame; Ruben Jaramillo, a peasant leader of the 1950s; and Florencio Medrano, the founder of the land occupation where we accompanied the poor. People had told us other stories as well, stories of leaders of the establishment who had been quietly "disappeared" by government forces. These were the outspoken prophets who found no way short of insurrection to change the systems of oppression that were destroying their people.

The stories of these heroes seemed larger than life. They championed the rights of the poor against corrupt and impossibly evil governments which protected the rich in their heartless exploitation of the poor. These leaders were anything but passive victims. They stood head and shoulders above the rest of us and recalled the heroism of Tom Payne, Ethan Allen, and Patrick Henry whom our American revolution had made famous. They were more like the dashing Anglo cowboy of our early movies than like the passive Mexicans.

Unconsciously, we had expected to encounter men and women of this stripe in Mexico. We had read of fraudulent election results, the marches protesting them, small insurrections in the mountains, and had even listened to Cuauhtemoc Cardenas in one of his speeches in Cuernavaca. Yet, the reality we discovered was far different. There were those among the middle-class intelligentsia who talked learnedly about theories of conflict and revolution, but the poor, who understood how precarious their position was and were in no hurry to put themselves and their families in jeopardy, did not. Revolution was a topic for expatriate Americans to discuss over cocktails but not a topic for the poor.

The poor struggle for justice because they are convinced that this is the plan of God that the rich have thwarted. To struggle for justice is a deeply-felt religious imperative. Still the poor show little interest in political doctrines or military maneuvers; they are a people of the concrete cause. When the government allows a concrete cause to emerge clearly, the poor will rise to challenge it. The Mexican government, however, is *muy listo*, very alert, and for seventy years has blunted or confused every cause that might underlie a revolution. Now that Mexican leaders are drawn more and more from the middle-class, which does not understand the poor and has allied itself with the business interests in the United States, it is possible, even likely, that they may miss an opportunity to weaken a cause for rebellion. The inflation the poor suffer today may be that cause.

So much for our unrealistic expectations born in the United States and based not on life as it is, but on life as the media imagines it to be.

The Reality

What we did discover, however, was more exciting, and because it was real, more challenging. The poor we met and have came to love are neither passive victims in love with their own suffering nor heedless heroes in quest of a new world order. They are men and women beginning to understand their own dignity as members of a persecuted community. As this understanding grows, they seek peaceful means to demand their rights as human beings and children of God. They are the backbone of society and the hope of a new future for Mexico and the whole Third World.

The base Christian communities, a host of cooperatives, the popular movement, and the better schools are training leaders who are beginning to find constituencies. As they do, a mighty force is forming, confused and disjointed now, but something to be reckoned with in the years ahead. If both the concrete cause and the leaders coalesce, revolutionary struggle will surely follow.

Having the "spirit of the poor" does bring happiness, as Jesus said. His society was also sharply divided between the rich and the poor. That spirit begins with an understanding of society itself. The poor understand, in a way we easily overlook, that the world is divided into the rich and the poor. No amount of striving, no amount of personal courage will change that. It may happen, but rarely does, that a few poor people may become rich or, even more rarely, that a few rich may become poor. It may even happen that an increase in wealth may bring about a situation in which a greater number escape poverty. Yet, in the minds of the Mexican poor, there is the belief that the world as we know it will continue much as it is now, short of a radical reappraisal of the goals that undergird it.

Unlike many North Americans, few Mexicans think of poverty as a product of their personal failure or as a punishment by God. They believe, as noted earlier, that their present anguish has been caused by an unregulated capitalism and a corrupt government whose officials enrich themselves at the people's expense. Their attitudes toward capitalism are based on the only capitalism they have known: a system of private ownership that has no concern, not even a publicly proclaimed concern, for the rights of the poor. In the face of this institutionalized greed, they long for a better system, based on justice and compassion. What that system should be remains a mystery, but they know that the present one is unfair and unjust. They have yet to evolve a clear alternative.

An Alternative Philosophy

Among those with the spirit of the poor, however, there are the seeds of an alternative philosophy based on a tribal past where communal ownership lived side by side with personal initiative. In their ancient villages, the community owned the land but allowed families to use parts of it as long as they farmed in harmony with the community. In this system, fathers could pass their right to their heirs, but the title to the land remained in the hands of the community, which served as the final judge of its use.

This ancient system was cruelly dashed by the Spanish conquerors in most parts of Mexico. Native Americans were enslaved, tribes annihilated, and a new layer of professional exploiters, called *caciques*, were created to govern them. For 500 years, the poor have been slaves or near-slaves to a few rich families, first those from Spain and later their descendants. Early in this century a remarkable revolution occurred. The poor threw off the bonds that had controlled them for four hundred years. Their revolution preceded the much more famous Russian revolution and was led by men who themselves were poor.

In the 1930s the Mexican government attempted to revive and institutionalize the ancient ways by removing some lands from private ownership and placing them in *ejido* status. Each new president solemnly promises to speed up the process of distributing land to the poor, but the distribution never takes place. The conservative forces are stronger than those of the poor—at least, up to this point.

To those poor who have come recently from the countryside into the cities, this communal form of ownership lingers in their minds. Capitalism, as practiced here, is new to them. They openly wonder whether such a system which has so little place for the community and depends totally on actions of individuals can ever bring them justice. They suspect that their ancient forms of ownership are better and that capitalism is a recent import from a culture foreign to their aspirations, a system held in place by violence.

This longing for a more just social order is the bedrock of the spirit of the poor. It includes an incredible patience and a very real awareness of God in their daily lives. But beneath these qualities lie the longing for justice and a deep suspicion that capitalism will not bring either justice or human happiness. They are not troubled by the failure of the Soviet Communist experiment since it was as foreign to their ideals as Euro-American capitalism. They have an admiration for some aspects of the American character—its basic honesty, its efficiency, and its love of freedom— and so were never interested in some alliance with America's enemy. They would like to be like Americans in some ways, but not like us in our individualism, our aggressiveness, or our greed.

Base Communities

This unconscious dis-ease with the injustice of modern life is the soil nourishing the phenomenal growth of base Christian communities throughout Latin America. In these communities the poor reflect on passages from the Hebrew and Christian Scriptures and use them as a measuring stick with which to evaluate their own conditions. They first come to understand their dignity as children of God, which leads them to realize that God does not want them to live in such deprivation any more than they want it for their own children. Armed with these ideas, they begin to analyze their own situation and to identify the people and ideas that enslave them.

One of the early understandings most groups stumble upon is their own complicity in the system. For centuries they have believed, based on the teaching of their pastors, that God wanted them to bear their burdens and say nothing. Because they were so docile in the face of "God's will," the rich and powerful habitually exploited them with impunity. Many now realize that their docility was and is a part of the problem.

Another discovery is the importance of a community. They have been a part of a mass migration from the campo to the cities, which has destroyed traditional family, tribal, and village ties. There is no going back, since agri-business has replaced the small farm. What work there is can be found only in the cities. In their small communities there the poor form a bond with other believers from other parts of Mexico. This bonding, based on common faith and social conditions rather than on family or village ties, can be profound, a real foundation of their new lives, especially if official pastoral agents encourage them and explain that community, too, is the desire of God.

Analyzing the Scriptures in relation to their situation leads them beyond an appreciation of their dignity and the importance of the new communities they form. They begin to understand who their enemies really are. These enemies may be local, as in the case of truck drivers who refuse to deliver water to them without a bribe, or more distant, as in the case of a president who wins his election by fraud. The enemies may also be church leaders who pour the resources of the church into projects for the well-to-do and counsel the poor to bear their burdens.

The Chief Enemy

But the chief enemy lurking behind government, educational, and church officials is the rich. The poor understand that that concentration of wealth and power is the force that must be overcome if justice is ever to be done. To the poor, there is no place in the kingdom of God for those who do not have the spirit of the poor. The parable of Lazarus and the rich man is a favorite story for their reflection.

Many Latin American writers have captured these themes, expressing eloquently the people's longing for dignity, community, and justice. Rightly have the powerful understood that such longings are the death-knell to their dominant positions and their institutions. First World governments, including our own, have supported repressive regimes in order to crush the longings of the poor. Brazil, Argentina, Chile, Bolivia, Nicaragua, Guatemala, El Salvador, and Mexico are a few countries where "national security" has justified cruel repression.

Financial institutions and international business groups have joined in this repression. They have allied themselves with a few rich families in each country and with their help exploited the poor to a degree unheard of forty years ago. By and large the U.S. government has been no more than an instrument in their greedy hands. American taxpayers have paid for their cheap bananas and coffee by supporting repressive governments with their tax dollars.

The churches, too, have sensed in the restlessness of the poor a challenge to their power. The Vatican has used every stratagem imaginable to separate the official church from the concerns of the poor. They have repeatedly criticized the theology of liberation, silenced those who have spoken forcefully against abuses in the church and society, appointed "safe" conservatives to important bishoprics, and honored those who have ignored and even oppressed the poor. The Vatican has not been alone in its opposition to the poor's desire for liberation. Fundamentalist churches have set up missions all over Latin America and teach what was once common among Catholics: unquestioning submission to authority. These sects and these conservative Catholic officials are the darlings of repressive governments and of the international cartels that control so much of Latin American life.

The Road to Damascus describes the situation this way:

> God is on the side of the poor, the oppressed, the persecut-
> ed. When this faith is proclaimed and lived in a situation of
> political conflict between the rich and the poor, and when
> the rich and the powerful reject this faith and condemn it as
> heresy, we can read the signs and discern something more
> than a crisis. We are faced with a kairos, a moment of truth,
> a time for decision, a time of grace, a God-given opportunity
> for conversion and hope.[1]

Even those church officials who call for an "option for the
poor" or even a "preferential" option for them are, the poor insist,
not saying enough. To declare an option for the poor means that
the church will continue to be something other than the poor. This
seems to assume that the real church is of the rich, which will perhaps open its coffers to the poor. What the poor are beginning to
demand, and not without good biblical backing, is that the church
become the church of the poor.

Spokespersons for the poor ask why church leaders are rich, why
honors are given to the wealthy, why bishops and popes must be
invested with symbols of power and be addressed with honorific
titles, why so much of its doctrine is about power, and why the
poor are not recognized as full members of the church founded by
a poor prophet with the help of poor, uneducated fishermen.
Those, like the Franciscan priest Leonardo Boff, who have spoken
most forcefully to these topics have been silenced by authorities in
Rome. The poor, however, cannot be silenced and history and the
Bible seem to indicate that God hears their cries.

In the midst of World War II, Dietrich Bonhoeffer, the German
Lutheran theologian saw the modern world so clearly, wrote:

> The church is the church only when it exists for others. To
> make a start, it should give away all its property to those in
> need. The clergy must live solely on the free-will offerings of

their congregations, or possibly engage in some secular calling. The church must share in the secular problems of ordinary human life, not dominating, but helping and serving. It
must tell [people] of every calling what it means to live in
Christ, to exist for others.[2]

An Age of Martyrs

The poor understand what Bonhoeffer said and they know who
their opposition is. They smile when the elite pass by: clergy, government officials, commercial magnates. They are polite but beneath this veneer seethes a deep resentment and a desire for
change. The base communities are preparing a tinder that needs
only a spark to burst into flames. That spark will inevitably be
struck; it is only a matter of time. The present, however, is the
time for martyrs, men and women like Oscar Romero, the Jesuits
of El Salvador, the thousands "disappeared" in Brazil and Argentina, the Christians buried in hidden graves in Chile, the leaders
quietly disposed of in Mexico. One Guatemalan catechist spoke of
his class of nineteen. The other eighteen were murdered by the
Guatemalan army in the name of national security with weapons
supplied by the United States and Israel.

Many of the poor believe that this age of martyrs is the beginning of change, a change they identify with the coming of the
kingdom of God. This new age will be marked by justice, compassion, and a deep sense of belonging. Convinced that God has not
forgotten them, they repeat the ideas of people like Daniel Berri-
gan, who said, "There is a God and his name is justice."

Endurance

This deep-seated hope brings with it a remarkable endurance, an
almost playful piety, and a willingness to be content with small
gains.

The endurance is manifested in a thousand ways, from spending days without water to waiting hours in line for the simplest
medical attention. It is an endurance in the face of violence from

other poor people, from the rich and their servants in government, and even from nature itself. It is the endurance of the woman with a large growth in her uterus who cannot afford to have it removed. It is the endurance of the old woman whose children have all gone to the States to find work and left her sick and alone. It is the endurance of the man who is not allowed time off from work even though two of his family are dying. It is the endurance of mothers who watch their hungry children grow weaker.

Endurance has a grim ring to it, but not in the lives of the poor. They feel that God is with them in their everyday lives, as close to them as their spouse or children. They talk of God, of Jesus, and of Mary, who are a real part of their lives. When it is time for community celebration, this closeness explodes into music, dance, and other forms of witness to the reality of the divine. Joy is never far from their hearts and lips.

Yet, contentment with God and even a playful happiness with one another does not blind them to their need to work for change. Day in and day out, they labor to make their community a better place in which to live. They meet frequently, pray regularly, and struggle for justice at every opportunity.

This is the spirit of the poor: a belief in the reality of God, a hope for the future, and a love shown in endurance, playful piety, and struggle for change. We have found that spirit and must now discover how we can tune our own hearts to its melody.

—Chapter Twelve—

Establishing the Kingdom

We share our experiences about life in the United States and Canada. What do they mean to us in light of our new experience?

After our workday has ended, we sit together on our small roof patio talking, wondering what the experiences of the day mean. We now spend many of our nights in a rented room in La Nopalera, but this evening we need the quiet and peace our home can provide. It stands on a steep hill and we can see the city stretched out beneath us, lights glittering, radios blaring, children still playing in the alleys, and cars rushing about with commuters, shoppers, and business people. It is a time for reflection, a reflection that goes beyond our articulated thoughts and feelings. We are content and at rest. Our time here has blessed us, but there lingers another challenge: how to share that blessing with those we left behind in the United States. How can we give you a glimpse into the spirit of the poor that will have meaning for your life?

This chapter differs from the others in that its setting is not out among the poor but on our patio as we reflect with you about the meaning of our experiences: what they mean for us, and what they mean for you.

184

"So What?"

After all that has been said in this book, the chief question on your minds has to be "So what?" You have walked with us through the poverty of La Nopalera and Primero de Mayo, met our friends, attended base community meetings, shared the excitement of our celebrations, and grasped something of what it means to have the "spirit of the poor." Now you might wonder how to make all this practical at home, at your job, in your church, in your family.

The answer to this is not easy because it must stand somewhere between a vague generalization, which has no practical value, and something so concrete that it evokes the old legalism we Catholics have just escaped. To say only that people in the U.S. and Canada need a form of spiritual poverty is the kind of vague generalization that gives preaching a bad name. To say, however, that one must give 8.3% of one's income to the poor is so concrete that it mobilizes our human desire for security against a threatening challenge. We will have to avoid both these problems in our response to this question: "Can we North Americans taste and touch the reality of the 'spirit of the poor'?" The answer is important, for without that spirit of the poor one cannot enter the kingdom of God.

This is not the only context in which this question arises for us. About twice a month, we speak to and dialogue with groups of North Americans at a retreat center, different from the one we left early in our stay here. It is sponsored jointly by the monks of Weston Priory in Vermont and the *Misioneras Guadalupanas de Cristo Rey*, a Mexican Benedictine congregation of women. Here we share some of the stories in this book and are invariably asked what the experience of meeting the poor might mean for everyday life in North America.

Then, too, many of our friends and family come to Mexico and walk the streets of La Nopalera with us, visit the new cooperatives the poor are forming, meet our friends, and sometimes listen to the dialogues in the base Christian communities. They are deeply moved and wonder, too, what it could mean for them.

Our first attempt to respond took place before we came to Mexico in the Vermont village of Weston where we lived. We invited friends to our home to talk about life and the meaning the Bible gave to it. Not everyone invited was comfortable and many met with us no more, but over the years a community was born that deeply influenced all of our lives and still exists. We remain in contact with these people who, though at a distance, are an important part of our lives. With them, we struggled with the question, "How can we embrace the spirit of the poor?"

The First Step

To respond to this sincere question, we must begin with characteristics that the poor themselves possess: restlessness and discontent. This sounds so negative and even un-American that we hesitate to speak the words lest we appear wild-eyed prophets completely out of touch with the people. Yet, unless we are discontent, we cannot yearn for change, we cannot even consider alternatives to the way life is at present. To grasp the spirit of the poor is to participate also in their restlessness. To the degree that we are restless and discontent we are free.

The people in the base communities here sing a little tune that embodies their methodology:

Ver, pensar,
actuar es el methodo
para caminar.

To look and think
and act is the way
to move ahead.

Ver

We begin our self-examination simply by looking at our lives to see what is really there. At this stage, we avoid trying to understand why our lives are the way they are. We refuse to blame anyone, even ourselves, for what we see, or even to suggest that what we see in our lives is wrong. At this stage, we only describe what is actually there. This sounds so easy that we may want to get it over with in a hurry and rush on to what is more challenging, but that would destroy the whole process. We must take the time necessary to describe what our lives are really like, to see what is really there.

Let's imagine a couple describing their lives for the first time in a base community they have just discovered through their local church.

SARAH   I spend hours every day in the car. I get up running, making breakfast for everyone, trying to meet the school bus schedule, helping my husband as well, who has to be to work on time. When everyone is gone, I rush to get dressed and jump into the car to get to my part-time job, selling lingerie in a nearby mall. I work on a commission so I have to be alert and push the items the store manager has marked as important to sell.

I get out of work about the time the kids finish school and begin taking them and their friends to their after-school activities, which takes me up to early evening. I rarely have time to cook the way I'd like to, but no one seems to notice, least of all my husband, who is tired and withdrawn when he gets home. I spend the evening doing housework, keeping an eye on the kids who watch TV and argue much of the time.

One day is much like the next, full of activity. I enjoy most of it, love my husband and my children, and can't imagine my life much different from the one I live. I know there are world problems; I catch a glimpse of them during the nightly news, but I have no time to think about them. I go to church on Sunday and enjoy the peace and quiet I find there.

STEVEN   My life is much like my wife's. I rush out of the house each morning and drive 40 minutes to work where I have a job I really love. In fact, I almost live two different lives, one at work, one at home. Except for the money I make at work and spend at home, there is very little connection between the two. My job is expediting orders for the company. I take the sales representatives' orders and see to it that each customer gets exactly what was ordered. The work is always a challenge and the people who work with me are good folks. We have a lot of fun together.

My wife is right. When I come home I am tired and sometimes a little irritable. After supper, I like to watch TV and turn in early. Saturdays are for making necessary repairs at home, watching the kids' games, and sometimes working if things get behind at the office. I go to church on Sunday because it is the right thing to do. I was brought up that way.

These descriptions may seem superficial but we cannot expect more from those who are only beginning to describe their lives. When this process is repeated week after week and new ideas are introduced through the reading of the Bible and through listening to others, the descriptions will begin to broaden and deepen. People will begin to wonder about many parts of their lives and the lives of those around them. They will begin to take the news more to heart and to see the church as more important for them. This is a slow awakening process. It cannot be hurried and it takes place at different rates with different people.

The base community movement adds another dimension to this reporting: community. Here we listen to others describe their lives; it also provides a sounding board of listeners as we describe our own lives. In our example, the husband and wife hear others less content with their jobs or their salaries. Some describe serious problems with their children and one man confesses to a lingering problem with alcohol. Listening to others triggers questions in our couple, questions never before spoken aloud but pushed long ago into the corners of their minds to be coped with later.

Pensar

Thinking about our lives and the way we live is a fearful experience. It becomes even more frightening when we couple our analysis with the Bible, for this sets up a comparison that may not be at all flattering. In fact, our analysis may be so upsetting that we may want to run from it. At times like these, the community helps us remain steady and open to the challenges our minds and hearts hurl at us. Because other people we respect are encountering the same problems, we realize we are not alone.

Back to Sarah and Steven, the couple we met earlier. After describing her daily routine, Sarah noticed that she never prayed and, in fact, had no contact with God at all except a kind of comfortable, spiritual rest on Sunday morning at church. She wondered if other women experienced the same problem and if there were a way of uncomplicating her life.

As Steven recounted his story, he remembered reading somewhere that on one's deathbed no one ever said, "I wish I had spent more time at the office." He began to wonder why work had become so much more important than his family or any other aspect of his life.

In time, through a natural and normal process of questioning, people will begin to look for answers to questions like these. The answers will lead to deeper questions, which in turn will be answered, only to present more questions. The most important part of this process is that we feel free to question anything and be willing to consider any answer as at least possibly true before we discard it.

Reading the Bible in the context of describing our lives often sets our minds afire. Connections we had never noticed jump into focus; thoughts we had not entertained since childhood rush into our minds. Often what had seemed normal and natural becomes questionable at best, troubling, and perhaps wrong. People begin to notice connections between one part of their lives and another, the systems that manipulate their thoughts, and the reasons people behave so much alike.

Our imaginary couple begin to ask why they are so busy and so harried. They wonder aloud if they are sacrificing their happiness for a relatively small share of the financial pie. The husband asks why his work is so separate from his children's lives. Why is he so reluctant to take them to his job and show them what he does? The wife wonders why she works at all. Would it not be better, she wonders, to cook more carefully and to spend more time with the children than to crowd her schedule by working for money they do not really need? And so it goes, on a personal and family level.

After a time, the questions will rise above the personal and family levels to questions about our consumer system, our competitive way of life, our government's relationship with the rich and powerful, our church's inability to cope with people's real problems, and so on. These questions do not all come at once; their order and timing will differ from one person to another, which must always be respected.

All through this process of describing and questioning, a mysterious thing is happening. What began as a group of individuals becomes over time a community of friends. This does not happen quickly, because we North Americans are a very individualistic people. Yet, the weekly discussions and self-revelations encourage a deep bonding. Individuals wonder how their lives are affecting others and how they can help others in their community with problems that are uncovered. This bonding, this building of community, takes place slowly and unevenly but it does happen.

Actuar

The easiest part of the process is the actions, which flow from the descriptions and analyses. At first they will tend to be individualistic, but with the growth of the community and the realization that many of our problems are shared in common, actions will move toward group actions. Once more, the process will be gradual and natural, happening perhaps without anyone ever noticing it.

The descriptions (*ver*) will deepen as people come to understand how much there is to see in their lives. The thoughts and analyses (*pensar*) will widen to include the whole human community and what is causing it to suffer so. The actions (*actuar*) will become more and more radical. As time moves on and people are faithful to the method, they will discover the place where the poor already stand, immersed in restlessness and dissatisfaction.

Stopping Short

The method is the work of a lifetime. In fact, it is the mission entrusted to believers by Jesus, the reason the Spirit of God came to dwell in our hearts, the whole purpose of church and of the Jesus movement in history. It is an intensely personal reality, because it calls for the conversion of hearts—but it is societal as well, because the Bible demands a time of justice, peace, and harmony among peoples, which it calls the reign of God.

In that summary of Jesus' teaching that Matthew remembered with such vividness (4:17), there were two distinct proclamations. The first was the word "repent." His hearers knew what this meant: changing their way of life, turning everything upside down, beginning life all over again, overturning their value system so that what was important became unimportant and what was marginal leaped to the center of their lives.

The early followers of Jesus' way were not surprised that they were thought of as subversives, were persecuted and even martyred. They knew that this repentance Jesus demanded marked them out for misunderstanding and living on the edge of society. They knew that what Jesus said was true: They could not serve Mammon and call this service the work of God, no matter how much piety surrounded it. They knew that even if the vast majority of people in their society held money, power, and prestige at the center of their lives, those who followed Jesus had to be different. If they were not with Jesus in this, the most important part of their lives, they were against him. They had to repent or remain in the way of life everyone else accepted. To be a Christian, then, was and is to be a radical, a man or woman living on the edge, counter-cultural.

The other proclamation of Matthew has always been at the root of Christianity: "The kingdom of heaven is close at hand." This kingdom is an epoch of human history when justice, compassion, and belonging will prevail. It is an earthly—not just heavenly—reality; it is what we can look forward to and must work to achieve.

In practical terms, what will the kingdom be like? It is a time when all workers will receive just compensation for their labor and can count on help for themselves and their families in times of need. A time when children will be given every opportunity for a good education. A time when the rich will pay a fair share of their taxes and medical care will be available to all. A time when the elderly will live out their lives in dignity. A time when husbands and wives will live in harmony and children will respect and love their parents. A time when consumerism and competition will die and the needs of the poorest will be met. A time when wars will cease and nationalism will crumble in the conviction that we are all sisters and brothers, members of God's single family.

When we begin from a place of restlessness and dissatisfaction, as the poor do, we long for change and are willing to struggle to achieve it, since we have nothing of value to lose. We easily turn to God to help us, knowing God's great concern for our welfare. We understand that our own efforts are limited and so we can relax and celebrate our smallest victories. To have this cluster of attitudes is to have the spirit of the poor.

The problem for those who have so much is to discover that they are dissatisfied and restless and to remain that way. To take a determined stance to remain that way for a lifetime will mark us as odd, ungrateful, unpatriotic, a challenge to others who are comfortable the way they are. We can expect to be isolated and disliked, thought foolish and unbalanced, rejected and even persecuted. As Jesus reminded us, the prophets had the same problem.

Not everyone who goes to live among the poor stays there for a lifetime. It is a very attractive place for adolescents and young adults who do not yet have family responsibilities. Many of the young remain there for only a few years until a new career or the reality of family responsibilities tempts them to return to where they came from. A young American couple we know were leaders in the peace movement until people began to shun them and their children. It was too much to subject their young school-age children to this kind of subtle persecution. They gave up their discontent and, without realizing it, conformed to the norms of their middle-class friends and neighbors.

Some who have failed in the American competitive race pretend to love and embrace the poor, but at the first opportunity leave. A middle-class Mexican woman left the school system under pressure. For a while she was an outstanding crusader for justice until she was offered her old job back with a raise in salary. She stopped coming to meetings and was rarely heard from again.

Even many of the poor themselves rush from this uncomfortable place of dissatisfaction and restlessness for reasons that appear superficial. One man in La Nopalera was once a leader of those who opposed the system—until the ruling party offered him a new Volkswagen van. He accepted the van and became a staunch supporter of the status quo.

These stories remind us of the parable of the sower and the seed (Matthew 13:4-9). How often we have interpreted this parable to mean being steadfast in religious things, in keeping a set of moral rules, or even of maintaining some abstract notion of faith! Put this parable in the context of the rest of Jesus' teaching about the reign of God and such interpretations seem washed out. To stand in the place of the poor and to remain there is something quite different, very challenging, and ultimately the only attitude that will change our lives completely.

The struggle to remain faithful to Jesus is more than most of us can accomplish by ourselves. Prayer will help, of course, but equally important is a community of believers who experience the same difficulties we do. The emotional support we receive from others with values like our own strengthens our resolve and convinces us that by placing God at the center of our lives we have not lost our balance.

Those who remain faithful accomplish remarkable things. In Mexico we have met groups of poor uneducated people who are changing their small world. There are groups of artisans and tradesmen who have formed cooperatives, women teaching other women how to sew and to cook more nutritious meals, neighbors forming child-care programs, families struggling for safe drinking water, groups providing basic health, education, and so on. In Vermont, our base community marched against war, visited the elderly and sick, opened our homes in hospitality to others, and time and again came to the aid of a family of Guatemalan refugees who lived nearby. In both Mexico and Vermont, we met people who understand that the reign of God is at hand, that they are to work to hasten its arrival, to make it more of a reality.

The Overflowing Cup

What is it like to live in the place the poor have hallowed? Jesus answered that question with a short litany of teachings that describe a life lived in the place the poor call home. If we fill our hearts with the restlessness and willingness to change that the poor possess, we will live:

In a land of gentleness
where we seek the best for the community
rather than for ourselves,
where competition and consumerism have no place
and the environment God created for all creatures
will be secure from our rapaciousness and violence.

"Happy are the meek, they shall own the earth."

In a place where we care so deeply
and feel such dissatisfaction and restlessness

that we sit at the bier of our civilization
and mourn the wars it has waged,
the children it has killed,
the aged it has forgotten,
the lakes and rivers it has destroyed,
and the poor it has condemned to death.

"Happy are those who mourn, they shall be comforted."

In a place where,
like the rest of the poor and powerless,
we long for a better world.
So great is our longing
that it is like the hunger of the starving peasant
or the thirst of the mother
who cannot give a cup of water to her child.

"Happy are they who hunger and thirst for justice,
     they shall be comforted."

In a place where we share so completely in a human community
that we touch the *hesed*, the healing love, of God,
a love so complete and so total that it heals,
the love the ancients called God's mercy.
It is a love that heals individuals,
societies, and the environment itself.

"Happy are the merciful, they shall find mercy."

In a place where suffering so purifies our heart
that it longs for justice
with a passion and a focus
only the poor
and the God who loves them
can understand.

"Happy are those with a pure heart, they shall see God."

In a place where the tenor of our lives,
like the lives of those around us,
is a struggle for justice
and the peace that follows it.
We do not compete.
We do not consume what we do not need.

"Happy are those who work for peace,
    they shall be called the children of God."

In a place where we are counted marginal,
odd and outside the world's interest.
Like others who count so little,
we become expendable and are easily disposed of
for we have become the world's poor.

"Happy are those persecuted in the struggle for justice,
    the kingdom of God is theirs."

This is what it means to have the "spirit of the poor," to stand
in their shoes, to breath their air, to live their lives, to see the
world as they see it. This is quite possible even for those who live
amid First World affluence. In fact, Jesus says that we must live
with "the spirit of the poor" if we are to enter the kingdom of
God. It is not a matter of choice, an ideal held out only for the
more religious among us or those who work for the church. It is
the way of life, the lifestyle, that marks the follower of Jesus.
There is no way to follow him other than to stand in the place of
the poor and to know their restlessness and desire for change.

This desire to follow Jesus into the place of the poor will be
misunderstood. We will be ridiculed, insulted, and even persecuted. Perhaps worse, we will be ignored. Jesus foresaw this (Luke
6:22-23):

Blessed are you when people insult you
  and persecute you
and speak all kinds of evil against you
  because you are followers of mine.
Be glad and rejoice
  for a great reward is yours.
This is how people treated the prophets
  who went before you.

For many centuries, those Christians who wished to bind themselves together as religious communities in order to follow Jesus
have solemnly promised one another to live as the poor do, to
love no one more than God, and to remain ever alert to God's
whisperings in their hearts. With the passage of time, these simple
promises were reduced to meaningless legalisms and often hidden beneath the verbiage of a piety that extolled conformity and
convenience. This marked a great loss to the church for in these
three promises lie the kernel of the Christian message, a challenge
to all who follow Jesus, the rich and the poor, the married and the
unmarried, educated and uneducated, priests and prophets,
women as well as men.

All of us are called to stand in the place of the poor and see life
as they see it, to love God above all things, and to obey every challenge God has laid upon our hearts. This is what it means to repent and work for the kingdom which is close at hand.

Ending the Day

The sun has set as the city lights illuminate the sprawl beneath us.
A moment of intense peace arrives with the onset of night. It is
time for rest. Tomorrow we will stand with the poor again and
see realities not seen before. With them we will long for justice
and the coming of the kingdom. We will hear the whispers of revolution they hear in the Bible.

We sit overwhelmed and silent, each in our own private space,
talking to God about what we have discovered together. We pray

for clarity, steadfastness, and compassion. We ask for the gift of wisdom so that we may unmask injustice wherever we find it and replace it with fairness and love. We ask the Spirit of God to gift us with some share of the "spirit of the poor."

But now it is night and time to rest.

Postscript

Celebrating 500 Years

In 1992 the Western world celebrated the 500th anniversary of Christopher Columbus's arrival in the Americas, even though we know that other Europeans had come to these shores before he did. His coming was different, however, because he inaugurated what turned out to be a systematic European invasion and conquest of a whole hemisphere, perhaps the most dramatic change our world had ever seen.

Latin America, Africa, the islands of the Pacific, and Europe itself would never be the same again. The English and the French would easily subdue and devastate the Native Americans of the north and offer countless Europeans a chance to begin life anew in their place. The Spanish, the Portugese, and to a lesser degree, the Dutch, followed a similar policy in Latin America, except where the Native American population was so dense—in present-day Peru and Mexico—they were forced to dominate rather than exterminate.

If our roots are European, there is much to celebrate in 1992. Whether we live in Argentina, Canada, or between, the conquest of this land opened to our forebears unprecedented opportunities. If, however, we are descended from African or Native American stock, the past 500 years have been a nightmare, comparable to the worst cruelty of the U.S.S.R. under Stalin or Germany under Hitler.

From the riches of this new world, Europe extracted the wealth necessary to set it on the course of industrial development. This revolutionary way of life was exported to every country on the globe. Today the oil of the Middle East, the bananas of Central America, the copper of Zaire, the coffee of Brazil, the nitrates of Chile, and the gold of South Africa all pour into the industrial world to support a lifestyle unknown in earlier times. Meanwhile, the producers of these materials languish in a poverty even worse than their forebears knew. In a very real way, the conquest of the Americas set the scene for life as we know it today. It also began the exploitation of nature that has made the industrialized nations wealthy but has undermined the natural integrity of our planet.

Time cannot be retrieved. We live 500 years after Columbus and it is our age, not his, that we must evaluate and, if necessary, change. We can, however, examine, in the light of what we have already said in this book, three institutions that have greatly influenced these 500 years and ask ourselves what should be done to improve them.

The first is the economy. Five hundred years ago, a government aided by a few merchants and bankers controlled the distribution of wealth. In time, especially in England and the United States, a new breed of leader emerged, the industrialist. Gradually the role of the government was minimalized and the merchants, bankers, and industrialists became more powerful than the government itself. The role of government was reasserted in different ways in this century, from the Communism of the U.S.S.R. and Cuba, to the Socialism of Great Britain and Nicaragua, to the quiet restrictions on capitalists by President Franklin Delano Roosevelt in the United States.

Today a new element has entered the economic picture, the ecology, the preservation of an environnment suitable for life. Neither capitalists nor government officials have given adequate attention to the problems our industrialization is causing.

In the light of the past 500 years which saw the rise of slavery, racism, maldistribution of wealth, exploitation of natural resources, and warfare among competing nations, we must ask if there is not a better way to direct our economic forces so that all of God's children, those on the planet now and those yet to come, will receive a fair share of the world's resources.

The second institution to examine is the nation-state. When the age of European expansion opened, many believed that kings ruled by divine right. Few believe that today. Many of those who rule are the men and women who have been able to seize power and hold it by force. Some nations insist on elections as a way to legitimate authority. Most, however, either do not have elections at all or have them as a smoke-screen behind which to hide those who have seized power.

We have made progress in the past 500 years in securing the basic rights of individuals, at least in the industrialized nations. Our problems today, however, are such that no one nation acting alone can cope with them. A consistent network of cooperation between peoples is necessary. Multinational companies move from nation to nation to exploit natural resources and people. Drug dealers operate with near-immunity in one nation while they destroy the social fabric of another. Some nations are so poor that their populations starve to death while in others people worry about gaining too much weight. In the light of all this, we must begin to ask if the time for nations is not past. Is it not time to begin a new world order, one in which all the goods of this world are guaranteed to all who live on Planet Earth, without respect to where they live?

The third institution to consider in the light of the past 500 years is religion, particularly Christianity. The colonialist European nations that conquered the Americas, exploited Africa, and dominated much of Asia called themselves Christian; as often as not they bore Jesus' cross on their conquering banners. Churches and churchmen often were as much involved in the exploitation of others as were the most cold-hearted industrialists, bankers, or soldiers. What happened to Christianity as the champion of the downtrodden and the poor?

If the age of nations has passed, as seems to us true, then perhaps the age of organized religion, churches, is also at an end. Or, to put this more acceptably, perhaps the time for churches as we have known them is at an end. Is it not possible to envision communities of men and women, rich and poor, in charge of their own march in faith toward God? Is it not possible to have communities without the kind of bureaucracy that kills initiative, blesses only the powerful, and assists them in raping the powerless and the poor?

These are the questions that arise in our minds as these 500 years come to an end. In Latin America, many of the poor say that in 1992 they celebrate 500 years of struggle against the forces that have so nearly destroyed them: capitalism, unjust governments, and a church that has not stood by their side. We can, at least, join with them in the spirit of their celebration and let their causes be our own.

Notes

Introduction
1. Robert Bly, *Iron John: A Book About Man* (Reading, Mass.: Addison-Wesley, 1991), p. 221. Bly uses the story line of an ancient fairy tale to chart the steps of growth in a man's life. We found that many of his insights applied to women as well as to men.

Chapter One
1. A sketch of the life of Felipe de las Casas can be found in The *Dictionary of the Saints* (abridged ed.) by John J. Delaney (Garden City, N.Y.: Image Books, 1983), p. 107.
    2. This translation and many that follow are taken from *The Christian Community Bible*, 2nd ed. (Quezon City, Philippines: Claretian Publications, 1988). This is the favorite translation of base Christian communities in Latin America since its notes view the text through the eyes of the poor and oppressed of the Third World. Many passages in English present the ancient text in startling and different ways that cause readers to rethink their understanding of familiar passages.

Chapter Two
1. The statistics recorded here are from *The World Almanac* and *Book of Facts—1991* by Mark S. Hoffman, ed. (New York: Pharos Books), pp. 732, 765.
    2. Third World Christians, *The Road to Damascus* (Washington, D.C.: Center for Concern, 1989).
    3. *Ibid.*, p. 8.
    4. *Ibid.*, p. 26.
    5. Alfred T. Hennelly, ed., *Liberation Theology: A Documentary History* (Maryknoll, N.Y.: Orbis Books, 1989), p. 37.
    6. The schema is called the Values and Lifestyle Program, or more popularly VALS research. A good overview of the study is available in *The Nine American Lifestyles* by Arnold Mitchell (New York: Warner Books, 1983). It has been applied to religion in the U.S. in *U.S. Lifestyles and Mainline Churches* by Tex Sample (Louisville: Westminster/John Knox Press, 1990).
    7. Sample, *op. cit.*, p. 109.
    8. Alan Riding, *Distant Neighbors* (New York: Alfred A. Knopf, 1985), p. 364.

Chapter Three
1. *Cantemos en Comunidad*, Comision de Musica y Liturgia (Cuernavaca: Diocesis de Cuernavaca), p. 194.

2. Opening address to the Latin American Episcopal Conference at Puebla in 1978, III, 3, quoted in *The Power of the Poor in History* by Gustavo Gutierrez (Maryknoll, N.Y.: Orbis Books, 1983), p. 136.

3. Given the long history of Christian persecution of the Jewish people, we are rightly sensitive to any thought that might appear to justify the pogroms and death camps of our past. This text in no way justifies such actions or attitudes, nor can it support any form of anti-Semitism. Peter was himself a Jew as were the members of the early church, and Jesus too for that matter. Peter's words were addressed only to that whole class of his compatriots who actively or passively, through outright plotting or through accepting the benefits that followed upon Jesus' death, participated in the rejection and condemnation of the Savior. Naturally, Peter's condemnation was valid only during the lifetime of those who themselves had participated in the events and has no relevance for later Jewish history. It is a parallel to the Jewish condemnation of the Egyptians in the time of Moses. Just as no one would today persecute the Egyptians for their rejection of Moses, so persecution of Jews for what happened 2000 years ago is absurd. What both stories can teach us, however, is that groups find it difficult to accept anyone who calls for change and often persecute these men or women rather than face up to their message.

4. *Centesimus Annus* by Pope John Paul II (Washington, D.C.: U.S. Catholic Conference, 1991), no. 62.

5. Riding, in *Distant Neighbors*, has many interesting bits of information on birth control, changing government policies on family size, abortion, and the role of the Catholic church. Consult the index under "birth control," "family," and "population."

6. Peter J. Donaldson, *Nature Against Us: The United States and the World Population Crisis, 1965-1980* (Chapel Hill, N.C.: University of North Carolina Press, 1991). Another plausible reason for U.S. government concern for birth control in Third World countries is "national security." With world population growth centered in the Third World, many predict that these poor countries will soon become restless under the neocolonialist domination they experience from the U.S., Europe, and Japan. While the First World has the technological means to defeat any revolution among the poor, the economic cost to the rich nations would be disastrous.

7. The statistics quoted here are from *Estado de Morelos* by José Lopez Portillo, an unpublished monograph very popular among social workers in Cuernavaca, the statistical information of which comes from various government reports.

Chapter Four

1. As with all things Mexican, it is difficult to distinguish the reality from the words the government uses to describe it. Mexican schooling is improving in some respects. More children attend school for longer periods of time. The government does provide a popular adult education program for those who have never completed *primaria* (grade six) or *secundaria* (grade nine). The economic situation, however, is affecting these

programs adversely since teachers are poorly paid, have few teaching materials available, and school buildings must support two sessions daily. Students attending the afternoon shift often do not finish school until 7:00 P.M. In addition, the teachers and administrators are themselves products of the same beleaguered school system and consequently are often ill-prepared to pass on the skills all effective education depends on. Finally, the Mexican population has grown so rapidly (900% in this century) that it would be difficult for any government education program to keep pace. A sensitive and realistic evaluation of the Mexican educational situation and its place in national politics can be found in *Distant Neighbors*.

2. This sermon was quoted in the journal of the famous Bartholomé de Las Casas who prevailed upon the king and queen of Spain to outlaw Indian slavery in the Americas. It is preserved in *Cross and Sword* by H. McKennie Goodpasture (Maryknoll, N.Y.: Orbis Books, 1989), p. 11.

3. Hennelly, *op. cit.*, p. 129. Since the disintegration of the Soviet empire, first in Eastern Europe and then in the Soviet Union itself, many have begun to believe that no alternative to capitalism exists today. More perceptive minds are insisting that what has failed in the Soviet Union is not Marxist communism but a kind of state capitalism introduced not by Marx, but by Lenin and Stalin. The problem with communism may be that it has yet to be tried, as Chesterton sagely remarked was true of Christianity.

4. Third World Christians, *op. cit.*, p.18.

5. Dorothee Solle, *Thinking About God, An Introduction to Theology* (Philadelphia: Trinity Press International, 1990), p. 103.

6. Howard Zinn, *The Twentieth Century: A People's History* (New York: Harper & Row, 1984), p. 110.

Chapter Five

1. Goodpasture, *op. cit.*, pp. 23-24.

2. Gutierrez, *op. cit.*, p. 53.

Chapter Six

1. Quoted in Hennelley, op. cit., p. 76.

2. Nora Aburto, *et al. Kairos Central America: A Challenge to the Churches of the World* (New York: Circus Publications, 1988), nos. 55, 56.

3. A short description of Aztec religion and the part it played in the conquest of Mexico can be found in *The March of Folly* by Barbara W. Tuchman (New York: Ballantine Books, 1984) pp. 11-12.

4. Third World Christians, *op. cit.*, p. 11.

5. Quoted in Hennelley, *op. cit.*, p. 73.

6. Solle, *op. cit.*, p. 153.

Chapter Eight

1. Bartholomé de Las Casas, quoted in Goodpasture, *op. cit.*, p. 9.

2. Robert Bly, *op. cit.*, p. 141.

3. Mircea Eliade,*The Sacred and the Profane: The Nature of Religion* (New York: Harcourt, Brace and World [Harvest Books], 1959), p. 14.

4. Robert Bly, *op. cit.*, p. 142.
5. Pope John Paul II quoted in Gustavo Gutierrez, *op. cit.*, p. 139.

Chapter Nine
1. Eliade, *op. cit.*, p. 165.
2. Thomas Merton, *Conjectures of a Guilty Bystander* (Garden City, N.Y.: Doubleday, 1966), p. 142.
3. Third World Christians, *op. cit.*, p. 12.
4. *The Church in the Present-Day Transformation of Latin America in the Light of the Council* (2nd ed.), (Washington, D.C.: U.S. Catholic Conference Publications, 1973), quoted in Hennelley, *op. cit.*, p. 110.
5. "The Use of the Bible in Christian Communities of the Common People," a talk preserved in Hennelly, *op. cit.*, p. 21.

Chapter Ten
1. "Christians for Socialism," quoted in Hennelly, *op. cit.*, p. 148.
2. Gustavo Gutierrez, *op. cit.*, p. 8.
3. Penny Lernoux, *The People of God: The Struggle for World Catholicism* (New York:Viking /Penguin, 1989) p. 153. Lernoux backs up her contentions with statistical studies. She notes that every hour 400 Latin Americans convert to Pentecostal or other fundamentalist churches and that one-eighth of all Latin Americans belong to these sects.
4. Oscar Romero quoted in *The Religious Roots of Rebellion* by Philip Berryman (Maryknoll, N.Y.: Orbis Books, 1984), p. 391.
5. *Ibid.*, p. 391.

Chapter Eleven
1. Third World Christians, *op. cit.*, p. 13.
2. Dietrich Bonhoeffer, *Letters and Papers from Prison*, enlarged ed. (New York: Macmillan, 1971), p. 382.

Selected Bibliography

Every bibliography is of necessity selective. A list of all the books that relate to Latin America and the culture of poverty would require a book of its own. We have listed here some of the more important and readable resources, which will help the reader understand more about Mexico, Latin America, and the lives of the poor. We have included background material, contemporary Latin American theology, and some fiction, which often says more than other literary forms about the reality of daily life.

1. Background

Eliade, Mircea. *The Sacred and the Profane: The Nature of Religion*. New York: Harcourt, Brace & World, 1959.

Gandy, D. Ross. *Twenty Keys to Mexico: Door to Latin America*. Cuernavaca: Bilingual Center for Multicultural Studies, 1990.

Levy, Daniel and Gabriel Szekely. *Mexico: Paradoxes of Stability and Change*. Boulder, Colorado: Westview Press, 1983.

Lewis, Oscar. *Five Families: Mexican Case Studies in the Culture of Poverty*. New York: Basic Books, 1959.

_____. *A Death in the Sanchez Family*. New York: Vintage Books, 1969.

_____. *The Children of Sanchez*. New York: Vintage Books, 1961.

O'Gorman, Frances. *Hillside Woman*. Rio de Janeiro: Ecumenical Center for Action and Reflection (CEAR), 1985.

_____. *Down to Earth*. Rio de Janeiro: CEAR, 1987.

Oster, Patrick. *The Mexicans: A Personal Portrait of a People*. New York: Harper & Row, 1989.

Paz, Octavio. *The Other Mexico: Critique of the Pyramid*. New York: Grove Press, 1972.

Riding, Alan. *Distant Neighbors: A Portrait of the Mexicans*. New York: Alfred A. Knopf, 1966.

208 WHISPERS OF REVELATION

Stein, Stanley J. and Barbara H. *The Colonial Heritage of Latin America: Essays on Economic Dependence in Perspective.* New York: Oxford University Press, 1970.

Theology

Aburto, Nora, et al. *Kairos Central America: A Challenge to the Churches of the World.* New York: Circus Publications, 1988.

Berryman, Phillip. *The Religious Roots of Rebellion: Christians in Central American Revolutions.* Maryknoll, N.Y.: Orbis Books, 1984.

Boff, Leonardo. *Jesus Christ Liberator.* Maryknoll, N.Y.: Orbis Books, 1978.

_____. *Liberating Grace.* Maryknoll, N.Y.: Orbis Books, 1979.

Goodpasture, H. McKennie. *Cross and Sword: An Eyewitness History of Christianity in Latin America.* Maryknoll, N.Y.: Orbis Books, 1989.

Gutierrez, Gustavo. *The Power of the Poor in History.* Maryknoll, N.Y.: Orbis Books, 1983.

_____. *A Theology of Liberation.* Maryknoll, N.Y.: Orbis Books, 1973.

Hennelly, Alfred T., ed. *Liberation Theology: A Documentary History.* Maryknoll, N.Y.: Orbis Books, 1990.

Lernoux, Penny. *Cry of the People: The Struggle for Human Rights in Latin America.* New York: Penguin Books, 1982.

_____. *People of God: The Struggle for World Catholicism.* New York: Penguin Books, 1989.

Scharper, Philip and Sally, eds. *The Gospel in Solentiname.* Maryknoll, N.Y.: Orbis Books, 1976.

Sobrino, Jon, S.J. *Christology at the Crossroads.* Maryknoll, N.Y.: Orbis Books, 1978.

_____. *The True Church and the Poor.* Maryknoll, N.Y.: Orbis Books, 1984.

Solle, Dorothee. *Thinking About God: An Introduction to Theology.* Philadelphia: Trinity Press International, 1990.

Third World Christians. *The Road to Damascus: Kairos and Conversion.* Washington, D.C.: Center for Concern, 1989.

Fiction

Allende, Isabel. *Eva Luna.* New York: Atheneum, 1989.

_____. *The Stories of Eva Luna.* New York: Atheneum, 1991.

Fuentes, Carlos. *The Old Gringo.* New York: Farrar, Straus & Giroux, 1985.

_____. *Terra Nostra.* New York: Farrar, Straus & Giroux, 1976.

Jennings, Gary. *Aztec.* New York: Avon Books, 1980.

Marquez, Gabriel Garcia. *One Hundred Years of Solitude.* New York: Harper & Row, 1970.

_____. *In Evil Hour.* New York: Harper & Row, 1970.